1980

Advent at the Gates:
Dante's Comedy

Advent at the Gates:
Dante's Comedy

BY MARK MUSA

INDIANA UNIVERSITY PRESS   BLOOMINGTON & LONDON

Publication of this book was assisted by
the American Council of Learned Societies
under a grant from the Andrew W. Mellon Foundation.

Published in Canada by Fitzhenry & Whiteside Limited,
Don Mills, Ontario
Manufactured in the United States of America

Library of Congress Cataloging in Publication Data
Musa, Mark. Advent at the gates.
1. Dante Alighieri—Criticism and interpretation.
I. Title. PQ4390.M86 851′ 72—21243
ISBN 0-253-30140-8

Reproductions used by courtesy of the Vatican Library.

For
Marco
Massimo
and
Marc' Andrea

Contents

Preface

With the exception of Chapter III, which was published in an earlier form some years ago, none of the material in this volume has appeared before. That the studies included are published for the first time as a book instead of separately as articles is partly due to my experiences as a teacher of the *Divine Comedy*. The cantos that are treated here are those that have provoked the greatest interest in my students. Over the years, as the discussions continued (and more and more interrelations between the cantos emerged), the chapters slowly took shape. And because, to a large extent, they reached a final form together, I am presenting them together.

I am grateful to the John Simon Guggenheim Memorial Foundation for the fellowship in 1972 that enabled me to finish the work.

Introduction

Of the many colorful figures in the *Inferno* (Francesca da Rimini, Farinata, Pier delle Vigne, Brunetto Latini, Pope Nicholas III, Ulysses, Guido da Montefeltro, Bertran de Born, Maestro Adamo, Ugolino) whose evocation casts a spell upon the reader, there are three, in my opinion, whom Dante has chosen to present ambiguously, whose personalities invite close, even suspicious analysis. Everyone today would probably agree as to the ambiguity in the case of Francesca; many, in the case of Ulysses; I, myself, consider the poet's treatment of Guido to be equally, if not more, tantalizing (and I am still attempting to discover what Dante wants us to believe about the last two figures). I offer here my attempt at deciphering the character of Francesca as one illustration of the type of problem involved in such cases.

The story of Francesca da Rimini and Paolo Malatesta, even reduced to its sober, factual details, is made to order for inspiring our sympathies, and Dante the poet has used all the artistry at his command to create one of the most moving stories that has ever been told. And it has suited his purpose to allow Francesca to present herself, on the surface at least, as utterly charming. If the Pilgrim was seduced by the gracious, aristocratic, tenderly and passionately eloquent, and oh, so feminine Francesca, so have been certain critics of the *Divine Comedy*. But the more one rubs away the surface of this charming image the more one must become suspicious of the picture that Francesca da Rimini is taking pains to give of herself.

But I do not begin my study of *Inferno* V with the figure of Francesca. Dante the poet has postponed the entrance on stage of Paolo and Francesca until the second half of the canto. What we first see is an indiscriminate representation of the totality of the damned whom the bestial Minos sentences with his tail. Then we pass beyond into complete darkness and into the fury of howling winds and screaming voices. A definition of the sin of Lust is given by Virgil and, as masses of the Lustful pass by shrieking in the air, he identifies them for his ward, beginning with the most depraved woman in history, in a list of more than a thousand names. Thus, before Francesca and her lover appear on stage, Dante has devoted the first half of the canto to a description of the stage itself, of the background against which she will appear; it is the reader's introduction to the realm of Hell proper, and as such should be studied carefully. Because this important section of the canto has so often been passed over quickly by readers, I have devoted more than half of my first chapter to the poet's reconstruction of the world in which Francesca is doomed to live, as this world is presented to the eyes of the Pilgrim, who has yet to meet the first sinner condemned to Hell, and who does not know that he is waiting for Francesca.

For aesthetic reasons, too, it is fitting to dwell at some length on the opening half of the canto: *Inferno* V is one of the only two cantos which can be divided thematically into two halves (the other is *Inferno* XIX which I treat in Chapter V). Between the two perfect halves there is a central tercet of transition which already contains a hint of the vast difference of the atmosphere that permeates the second half. No longer the cries of the damned; an atmosphere now hushed in tranquillity, the sound of one tender voice. And as attention is focused on one individual, the tone of cold impersonality that characterized the description of the Lustful *en masse* and the definition of the nature of their sin give way to the warmth of a personal confessional mood. Finally, while in the second half the time is clearly that of the present, and we are offered staged activity taking place before our eyes—in the first half Dante the poet has made it very difficult for the reader to know where he is in time, and whether what is described so vividly (and the descriptions here are much more vivid than those in the latter part) is an event taking place at the moment or a phenomenon eternally recurring. It would seem that the Pilgrim observes certain things and learns about many others. The reader is offered all of this together and must learn to distinguish the one from the other. He will think he has his feet on the stable ground of the present moment only to find that he has been caught up in the mechanics of eternity. That the poet should wish to manipulate these two levels of time in his first presentation of the Pilgrim in Hell is not difficult to understand, once this poetic device is divined. After describing the atmosphere of the Second Circle and pointing to the lessons which this suggests, I return once more to the appearance of Francesca on stage, concerning myself only with the reaction she produces on the Pilgrim, in whom Virgil had been trying to instil the proper attitude toward Lust.

In at least three ways Canto XIX, dealing with the sin of simony, particularly as embodied in Pope Nicolas III, is reminiscent of Canto V. Again, a canto falls into two exact halves, corresponding, here, to two stages in the development of the Pilgrim. In both cantos, again, a lesson is offered to the Pilgrim: while in V he fails to assimilate it, in XIX he succeeds splendidly. In fact, not only does he come to understand the nature of Simony as he had failed to understand that of Lust: he also understands what Virgil has tried to teach him about sin in general: that, among the damned, individual traits cease to be significant.

Finally, there are no other cantos than V and XIX in the *Inferno* with such a heavy concentration on the nature of the sin involved and on its results. In every canto, of course, the particular punishment meted out to the sinners is described in greater or lesser detail, but it may happen that the sin itself is not mentioned and that there is nothing made explicit in the narrative or the conversation to remind the reader of it, as in the cantos of the Sodomites (XV, XVI). Frequently we are offered Virgil's identification of various sinners, sometimes accompanied by a brief denunciation; again, the sinner himself will mention his sin in passing, or offer accusations against other sinners; occasionally he will imitate his sin while taking part in the action of the canto. In only one case are we constantly reminded of the sin throughout the canto—in the treatment of Sorcery (XX) where eight historical figures are pointed out, and one of

them (Manto) is described at considerable length for the sole purpose of telling the story of the founding of Mantua. And only once
does the author himself intervene to condemn the sin: in Canto XII
where the "Violent against others" are punished (49–51).

It is in the second part of Canto V that we feel most strongly
the poet's thoughtful concern about the sin of lust. In the first part
we are twice reminded of the punishment of the Lustful, and a
brief definition of their sin is offered by Virgil: on the surface, at
least, it offers hardly more in its treatment of sin than many other
cantos. But in the second half Dante the poet has done what he will
never do again: he has allowed a sinner to relive, for the reader's
sake, her experience of temptation and of final compliance, allowing
her also to justify her sin and to tempt the reader into sympathy,
thereby illustrating the insidious force of seduction that makes man
"submit reason to desire."

In Canto XIX not once but twice is heard the voice of Dante the
poet in veritable explosions of intense concern about the hateful sin
of simony and its punishment. The canto begins with a two-tercet
apostrophe to Simon Magus, and hardly is the narrative resumed
when there is a second outburst, this time of admiration for the
Divine Justice that has devised such a fitting castigation of Simony.
Again, it is in the second half that the nature of the sin of simony is
most elaborately revealed: to some extent in the words of Nicolas
who callously describes his own sins and those of his successors, but
mainly in the Pilgrim's indictment of Simon and his congeners,
which has the same authoritative and passionate ring as the words
of the poet himself at the beginning.

All this is easily perceptible on the surface; beneath the surface,
there are two other indications of the poet's concern with the sin
in question. The interpolation, toward the beginning of the canto, of
the autobiographical incident involving the Baptistry of San Giovanni throws light, as I try to show, on the nature of the sin of
simony; and the description of the legs of Nicolas locked in his pit
reveal, when seen in connection with another canto of the *Inferno*,
the poet's horror of this sin. Just why Dante should choose to focus

so intensely on two sins as different as that of Lust, the least offensive to God, and that of Simony, which would destroy God's church,
this should not be too difficult to understand.

Chapters IV and V of this book must be seen somehow together.
Several years ago I published a brief article presenting my belief
that in Canto IX of the *Inferno* the climactic event narrated should
be interpreted as referring to the First Coming of Christ, and that
the parallel event in Canto VIII of the *Purgatory* was a prefiguration
of His Second Coming. Given these two cases of an exceptional
function of the narrative, it seems only logical to assume that the
author must have taken particular care in both cantos to prepare for
the representation of the Advent. In both cases, before the divine
messengers appear on stage, the reader is made to feel, more dramatically in the first case, more subtly in the second, a change of
atmosphere which leaves him disoriented. As Virgil stands helpless
before the Gates of Dis that have been slammed shut in his face, and
we hear the Furies' screams to Medusa offstage, it is as if we were
back in the Pagan World of centuries past. And Christ has not yet
come. In the Valley of the Princes, as we listen to the evening hymns
being sung by the ransomed souls asking for God's protection
against the Temptor and for Mary's intercession with Christ for
their salvation, we seem to be not in Purgatory but in a Christian
community on earth, a community waiting for the Daily Coming of
Christ. On the one hand, a shift of historical time is suggested, on
the other a shift of spiritual place involving time.

The effect of disorientation achieved in the cantos treating the
two Advents must remind us of the disequilibrium effected in the
first part of *Inferno* V, where the distinction between eternally
recurring phenomena and single actions in the present is blurred.
But there the effect was achieved in a different way: the poet simply
played a trick on the reader, withholding that minimal bit of explanation that would have allowed him perfect orientation. In
Inferno IX, however, and in *Purgatory* VIII it is the events themselves that are puzzling—including the psychological transformation of Virgil. At the same time, on the technical level of narration

the author is also playing tricks on the reader by withholding or delaying information, interfering with the smooth flow of narrative time. It is interesting that Dante should at times deliberately attempt to give us a confused or even a false view of the events taking place on the stage he has constructed, forcing the attentive reader (for only the attentive reader will know he is confused or off the track) to adjust his vision until he has achieved the proper focus. The reader should always welcome indications of "confusion" in Dante's procedure as a storyteller, believing that they must lead to the perception of a well-wrought clarity.

In the chapters so far discussed each of the cantos involved is studied as a whole and as a unit (sometimes with a view of what precedes and follows), with close attention to the development of the action contained therein. In the final chapter of this book I isolate for analysis a small section of the first half of Canto XXIV of the *Purgatory:* the conversation between Bonagiunta da Lucca and the Pilgrim who appears for the first time as "the poet in the making" and whose voice, perhaps, almost blends with that of the author of the *Divine Comedy* (reminding us faintly of the Pilgrim's words in *Inferno* XIX). Here, of course, there is no narrative and there can be no question of narrative technique in the usual sense. But in the sequence of commands and propositions and questions and propositions again there is illustrated a dialectic which demands the closest scrutiny.

After having given a brief summary of the commonly accepted interpretations of this passage, I offer a list of problems which I consider to be implied in this crucial conversation between two poets and which have been, so far, treated insufficiently by the critics. The attempt to answer the (twelve) questions suggested to me by the conversation in *Purgatory* XXIV sends us backward and forward in the *Divine Comedy* and even to another work by Dante. As a result I have been able to offer a new interpretation of the famous phrase *dolce stil nuovo* (upon which had been based the idea of a recognized school of poets contemporaneous with Dante), and to discover a new image related to the spiritual and poetic development of the Pilgrim, which his fellow poet had been able to begin to comprehend during his stay on the terrace of the Gluttonous.

The cantos chosen for analysis in this book offer excellent examples of Dante's narrative technique and his art of characterization. Because these are aspects of his genius in which I am particularly interested, my treatment of the cantos has been analytic rather than synthetic: my interpretations are the result of a very close, perhaps pedantically close, way of reading. In my general reading my habit is to assume whenever I come to a passage I do not find completely clear, that there are three possible explanations: the author is at fault; I, the reader, am at fault; or the author is deliberately challenging his reader. In my reading of the *Comedy* I always exclude the first possibility; as for the other two, perhaps they may be reduced to one: the reader who is confused is always at fault—in the second case he would have failed as a normal reader, in the third, as an "ideal reader."

And when I find myself puzzled over any detail of characterization or narrative, I consider it to be of the utmost importance to discover on which of the two planes I have failed. It usually takes little effort for a reader to recognize when he has been a simpleton and, in that case, the problem disappears immediately. But when that does not happen, when the reader, often after much concentration and rereading still finds himself confused, he can be rather sure that he is up against one of the not infrequent passages in which Dante the Poet is deliberately challenging him, hoping that his reader's clear-cut confusion will serve as a stimulus strong enough to force him to become, for the moment, the "ideal reader." As a matter of fact, there are two famous cases in which Dante has directly addressed his reader, calling upon him to see beneath the veil of the *strani versi.* Much more often he is silently asking his reader (by throwing him into confusion) to recognize that the moment has come for special effort.

It should go without saying that close reading and rereading may not only lead to clarification of the difficult but also to enrichment of the "easy." But in my case, I would say that most of what I offer that is new in this book has been the result of a long drawn-out failure to understand—of, I hope, a *felix culpa*.

Advent at the Gates:
Dante's Comedy

Phlegyas ferries Dante and Virgil across the Styx toward the City of Dis. Canto VIII, *Inferno*. From the Vatican, Biblioteca Apostolica, MS Urbino Latino 365. Guglielmo Giraldi and assistants, ca. 1478.

I

A Lesson in Lust

PREVIOUS studies of Canto V of the *Inferno,* brilliant though some of them have been, I have found mainly disappointing in three regards—all of them being the result of the spell cast by the charming young noblewoman of Rimini. In the first place, many critics have been so moved by the romantic tragedy of Paolo and Francesca, who appear in the latter part of the canto, that they have neglected the first part, which means, among other things, that they have failed to study the carefully wrought structure of the whole.[1]

Secondly, concern for the pair of lovers has led many critics to overlook the fact that the canto not only tells their story but also relates a most important episode in the story of the Pilgrim, who is the protagonist of the *Divine Comedy.* With Canto V, the process of his spiritual development has barely begun, most of his journey still lies ahead of him, and for the first time he will be allowed to witness, having arrived at the Second Circle, the spectacle of the damned being punished in Hell. We must wonder at the outset what his reactions will be to what he sees and hears: how much he will have learned by the end of the canto. Moreover, even those who do take an interest in the psychology of the protagonist often fail to distinguish clearly between Dante the Pilgrim, the fictional character, and Dante the Poet, who created him. As a result, they may attribute to the latter, to the artist-theologian, certain all-too-human attitudes that could belong only to the weak, confused, inexperienced Pilgrim.[2]

Thirdly, many of those who have limited themselves to offering an interpretation of the figure of Francesca (surely a valid, if partial, approach to this canto) have tended, precisely because they have been so easily fascinated by her charm, to treat her superficially, to take her at face value—instead of attempting to· penetrate beneath the charming surface she offers.

In my treatment of Canto V I intend to discuss all three of these neglected aspects: describing its structure, exploring the significant role played by the Pilgrim, and subjecting the figure of Francesca to an impersonal analysis. If only because this treatment involves consideration of two such complicated problems as the behavior of the Pilgrim and the behavior of Francesca (problems which should be studied separately before we can see the interaction between the one and the other), I shall devote two chapters to *Inferno* V. In the first I shall treat the Pilgrim (after a preliminary discussion of structure), in the second, the figure of Francesca.

Canto V falls perfectly into two halves, with a tercet of transition: 1–69; 70–72; 73–142. The first half, as we shall see later, consists mainly of explanations of the habitually recurring phenomena to be encountered in Hell; in terms of the actual events that take place, it can be very briefly summarized. At the entrance to the Second Circle the Pilgrim and his guide see the horrible figure of Minos, engaged in the performance of his infernal duties. The Judge of Hell immediately espies the intruders and, suspending temporarily his administration of Justice, hails the Pilgrim with menacing words—which are answered with severe contempt by Virgil. The monster being silenced, the two travelers, proceeding, enter into the space of the Second Circle,[3] where the Pilgrim hears a confusion of doleful sounds whose nature and whose cause Virgil explains to him. Finally, there comes into the Pilgrim's range of vision a flock of wailing spirits, and as they come closer, Virgil points out to him, and names, the members of the group.

Now let us go back to the beginning to examine the first half in greater detail. It falls, thematically, into three parts: 1–24; 25–45;

46–69 (24 lines; 21 lines; 24 lines). In the first the figure of Minos dominates. In line 4 we are offered a visual and an auditory impression experienced by the Pilgrim: he sees the hideous monster and he hears him snarl. The same combination of the visual and acoustic is present in lines 16-21: while looking at Minos he hears his threatening words and Virgil's reply. But in the intervening section, lines 5–15, there is recorded no sense-impression whatsoever; this offers not a description of on-stage activity taking place at the moment, but an explanation of the way justice is administered by Minos to each sinner that comes (that has come, that will come) before him:

> Stavvi Minòs orribilmente, e ringhia:
>   essamina le colpe ne l'intrata;
>   giudica e manda secondo ch'avvinghia.
> Dico che quando l'anima mal nata
>   li vien dinanzi, tutta si confessa;
>   e quel conoscitor de le peccata
> vede qual loco d'inferno è da essa;
>   cignesi con la coda tante volte
>   quantunque gradi vuol che giù sia messa.
> Sempre dinanzi a lui ne stanno molte:
>   vanno a vicenda ciascuna al giudizio,
>   dicono e odono e poi son giù volte.
> "O tu che vieni al doloroso ospizio,"
>   disse Minòs a me quando mi vide,
>   lasciando l'atto di cotanto offizio.... (4–18)

> (There stands Minos grotesquely, and he snarls,
>   examining the guilty at the entrance;
>   he judges and dispatches, tail in coils.
> By this I mean that when the evil soul
>   appears before him, it confesses all,
>   and he who is the expert judge of sins
> sees what place in Hell the soul belongs to;
>   the times he wraps his tail around himself
>   tells just how far the sinner must go down.

> The damned keep crowding up in front of him:
>> they pass along to judgment one by one;
>> they speak, they hear, and then are hurled below.
> "Oh you who come to the place where pain is host,"
>> Minos spoke out when he caught sight of me,
>> putting aside the duties of his office. . . .)

Just what action it was that Minos was in the midst of when the
Pilgrim caught sight of him we shall never know.[4]

But if section 5–15 contains not the immediate impressions of
the Pilgrim but information about habitual phenomena, it is also
true that this information is something that the Pilgrim could not
possibly have gained from his own observations up to this point. We
must assume, then, that he has learned it from his teacher. We may
easily imagine that, during their passage from the first to the second circle, Virgil prepared his ward for the figure he would see
immediately on their arrival, describing beforehand Minos' function and its mode of execution.

Assuming that this conversation did take place (and I know of
no other explanation),[5] it was most artful of the poet not to let us
overhear it, but to postpone the information in question until just
after the Pilgrim has caught sight of the infernal judge, thereby interrupting the narrative dealing with the on-stage action (which
has only barely begun). For one second we are by the Pilgrim's
side, staring with him at the snarling monster, *hic et nunc*. Then the
hic et nunc dissolves, as we learn about Minos' infernal duties, eternally executed at the entrance of the Second Circle, which is the
gateway to the punishment of sin. But the picture of Minos has remained etched in our memory while we are learning. "Stavvi Minòs
orribilmente, e ringhia" is perhaps the most powerfully descriptive
single line in the *Inferno*.[6]

Now, since Minos must stand at the entrance to Hell proper,
and since this entrance is also that of the Second Circle, Dante was
forced to treat, in the canto devoted only to Lust (the least offensive
of the sins punished in Hell), the figure of the judge who functions for all the circles, who passes judgment also on the blackest of

crimes. The poet was not, however, forced to put this figure into relief as dramatically as he did. And, if he has chosen to do so, this must mean that he wished to exploit the "necessity" of Minos' presence here for artistic purposes; for though the Second Circle is far away from the terrible depths of Hell, it is, nevertheless, Hell; and though Lust may be the least heinous of the capital sins, it is nevertheless sin. And because the reader, listening later to the tragic tale of the sweet Francesca, may be tempted to forget this, Dante would have him recall the hideous figure of Minos who, with his tail, pronounced sentence on Francesca as well as on Thaïs the whore.

In the second part of the first half of our canto basically the same device of interpolation is employed. In the first two tercets are described the (mainly acoustic) impression of the Pilgrim:

> Or incomincian le dolenti note
>   a farmisi sentire; or son venuto
>   là dove molto pianto mi percuote.
> Io venni in loco d'ogne luce muto,
>   che mugghia come fa mar per tempesta,
>   se da contrari venti è combattuto. (25–30)

> (And now the notes of anguish start to play
>   upon my ears; and now I find myself
>   where sounds on sounds of weeping pound at me.
> I came to a place where no light shone at all,
>   bellowing like the sea racked by a tempest,
>   when warring winds attack it from both sides.)

He hears first ("Or incomincian . . .") the wails of the tormented sinners; then only, the environmental noises. The one reference to vision is that of absence of vision (for which we were already prepared by the last line of Canto IV: ". . . loco d'ogni luce muto"). It is not until the opening tercet of the third part containing the all-important word "vidi" (48) that we are offered another sense impression of the Pilgrim. The five tercets in between (31–45)

contain information about timeless activity (and state). The first
two tercets of the informative interpolation (31–36):

> La bufera infernal, che mai non resta,
>> mena li spirti con la sua rapina;
>> voltando e percotendo li molesta.
> Quando giungon davanti a la ruina,
>> quivi le strida, il compianto, il lamento;
>> bestemmian quivi la virtù divina.

> (The infernal storm, eternal in its rage,
>> sweeps and drives the spirits with its blast:
>> it whirls them, lashing them with punishment.
> When they are swept back past their place of judgment,
>> then come the shrieks, laments and anguished cries;
>> there they blaspheme the power of almighty God.)

offer an explanation of the sounds the Pilgrim has just begun to
hear (with which the Second Circle continuously resounds), an
explanation involving the nature of the punishment inflicted upon
the sinners in this circle. In the next tercet (37–39) we are told who
these sinners are:

> Intesi ch'a così fatto tormento
>> enno dannati i peccator carnali,
>> che la ragion sommettono al talento.

> (I learned that to this place of punishment
>> all those who sin in lust have been condemned,
>> those who make reason slave to appetite.)

The final two tercets (40–45) offer to our imagination (not, of
course, to our sight) the appearance of the eternally tormented
sinners:

> E come li stornei ne portan l'ali
>> nel freddo tempo, a schiera larga e piena,
>> così quel fiato li spiriti mali

di qua, di là, di giù, di sù li mena;
  nulla speranza li conforta mai,
  non che di posa, ma di minor pena.

(And as the wings of starlings in the winter
    bear them along in wide-spread, crowded flocks,
    so does that wind propel the evil spirits:
  here, then there, and up and down, it sweeps them
    forever, without hope to comfort them—
    hope, not of taking rest, but of suffering less.)

The emphasis on the timeless is most obvious in the middle
tercet, which is concerned simply, factually, with the nature of the
sin that is punished (forever) in the Second Circle. But it should be
evident that also in the two that precede and the two that follow,
though they present a vivid description of sensuously perceptible
phenomena, we cannot possibly have to do, here, with sense impressions received by the Pilgrim (note the *Quando* of habitual activity
in line 34). Soon he will see certain spirits driven by the fury of the
infernal blasts. But at the point reached at the end of line 30, the
Pilgrim (once having passed Minos) has seen, as we know, nothing
whatsoever. To suddenly take for granted the presence of a group
of spirits (*li spirti,* line 32) within the range of the Pilgrim's vision
is impossible: the "spirits" casually mentioned in this line can refer
only to the totality of sinners present in the Second Circle. Similarly
"li spiriti mali" of line 42 which contains the first bird image, must
refer to the same indefinite totality of sinners.[7]

Again we must assume that the information contained in the
interpolation has been supplied by Virgil; indeed, as concerns the
central tercet introduced by the word *Intesi,* we are told as much:
the specification of the sin that is punished in the Second Circle, the
Pilgrim can have heard only from Virgil. And I suggest that the
Intesi with which the central tercet begins should be taken as anticipated in the two tercets that have preceded, and also should be
prolonged into the two that follow. And it is, of course, at the
moment described in lines 25–30, when the Pilgrim has begun to

hear the distant sounds coming from the unseen spirits and from the winds that torment them, that Virgil would have begun to teach him what we learn in the next five tercets.[8]

Why did the poet not make it immediately clear that this whole passage represents information supplied on the spot by Virgil— either by beginning with *Intesi* two tercets earlier, or by presenting Virgil as speaking before us, to the Pilgrim (e.g., *ed egli a me*)? And as for the earlier interpolation, describing Minos' function introduced in the first part (1–24), which contains no *Intesi,* we are not even given a hint as to the source of the Pilgrim's information, or as to when such a conversation as we have imagined between teacher and ward would have taken place. We may, of course, deduce from this (indeed, we must) that Dante wanted his reader to solve the problem of the source of information by himself. But even granting this and granting, of course, that the solution here proposed is the correct one, another problem still remains. Since in both cases the informative interpolation is introduced without warning, the reader must fall immediately into a trap (from which the commentators, apparently, have not been able to extricate themselves): anyone proceeding from line 4 ("Stavvi Minòs . . .") to line 5 ("Essamina le colpe . . ."), and again from line 30 (". . . contrari venti . . .") to line 31 ("la bufera infernal . . ."), must believe, at that moment, that he is reading a continuation of what has just preceded. At some point, however, if he is reading carefully, and if he has a sense for what can be on-stage activity and what cannot be, he will see that, without realizing it, he has passed from the step-by-step rhythm of "what happened next" to an explanatory summary of habitual activity, of eternal process. He will see that he has been tricked by the poet into eternity. Surely, the inevitable temporary shock produced by the poet's narrative procedure was willed for artistic reasons.

Whereas the first interpolation was concerned with the mode of passing sentence upon the sinners, the second describes the form their punishment assumes (at least for those in the Second Circle), and the reactions this provokes in them. Accordingly, in the picture of Minos, there was described activity performed: grim, resolute, vigorous, systematic activity, activity with a purpose;[9] in that of the condemned, buffeted by the winds, we have activity forced on the agents (the endless, aimless, disorientated movements through the air), or activity resulting from frustration and despair (the periodic, anguished screams). And the second interpolation distinguishes itself from the first also because of its clear-cut symmetrical proportions and the vividness of its imagery. Between the wild sounds and the wild movements described by Virgil is inserted the tercet of doctrinal implication revealing the stern meaning of the meaningless agitation. The first passage (31–36), offering an explanation of the confused sounds just heard by the Pilgrim (25–30), ends with the spirits' cries of blasphemy against "the Divine Power," thereby leading up to the specification of the sin for which they were damned by the Divine Power. Then, as if to show how appropriately the punishment fits the sin, the last two tercets, which are in balance with the first two, develop an image already latent there: that of a dense flock of birds with their swooping, darting, climbing movements—a pandemonium of wings.

If in the first part (of the first half of our canto) the role of Virgil as teacher was completely obscured, and in the second was only hinted at, in the third (46–69) we hear from his own lips the information he gives his ward: as a flock of the lamenting spirits of the lustful, compared to a long line of chanting cranes, comes within their range of vision (*vidi, venir* . . . : 48), the Pilgrim turns to his guide to learn their identity; and Virgil begins his list of more than a thousand names:[10]

> "La prima di color di cui novelle
>   tu vuo' saper," mi disse quelli allotta,
>   "fu imperatrice di molte favelle.
> A vizio di lussuria fu sì rotta,
>   che libito fé licito in sua legge,
>   per tòrre il biasmo in che era condotta.

Ell'è Semiramìs, di cui si legge
    che succedette a Nino e fu sua sposa:
    tenne la terra che 'l Soldan corregge.
L'altra è colei che s'ancise amorosa,
    e ruppe fede al cener di Sicheo;
    poi è Cleopatràs lussurïosa.
Elena vedi, per cui tanto reo
    tempo si volse, e vedi 'l grande Achille,
    che con amore al fine combatteo.
Vedi Parìs, Tristano"; e più di mille
    ombre mostrommi e nominommi a dito,
    ch'amor di nostra vita dipartille. (52–69)

("The first of those whose story you should know,"
    my master wasted no time answering,
    "was empress over lands of many tongues;
her vicious tastes had so corrupted her,
    she licensed every form of lust with laws
    to cleanse the stain of scandal she had spread;
she is Semiramis who, legend says,
    was Ninus' wife and successor to his throne;
    she governed all the land the Sultan rules.
The next is she who killed herself for love
    and broke faith with the ashes of Sichaeus;
    and there is Cleopatra who loved men's lusting.
See Helen there, the root of evil woe
    lasting long years, and see the great Achilles
    who lost his life to love, in final combat;
see Paris, Tristan"—then, more than a thousand
    he pointed out to me, and named them all,
    those shades whom love cut off from life on earth.)

In the first four tercets three famous women are presented. To Cleopatra one line is given; to Dido, who is not mentioned by name,[11] two lines; but Semiramis is given three complete tercets, for she is the first ("la prima di color di cui novelle/tu vuo' saper . . ."). Here, Virgil probably means "the first" in importance, the one most necessary for the Pilgrim to learn about; at any rate, if the

legends about her are true, the "lussuria" of Semiramis surely out-
weighed many times that of the other sinful women.[12] One more
woman is (briefly) mentioned, Helen of Troy; then follow the
names of three men.[13]

The inequality in the number of lines assigned to the different
figures named suggests, as has been said, a hierarchical distinction
of degrees of infamy, but it also serves an aesthetic end: the movement slowly begun with Semiramis becomes quicker and quicker
(at the conclusion, Paris and Tristram must share a hemistich), to
end with a dizzying succession of innumerable illustrious names (or,
so it must have been for the Pilgrim; we the readers are not allowed
to hear the rest).[14]

The description of the multitude of lustful sinners leads
smoothly into the central tercet of the canto which describes the
Pilgrim's reaction:

> Poscia ch'io ebbi 'l mio dottore udito
>   nomar le donne antiche e' cavalieri,
>   pietà mi giunse, e fui quasi smarrito. (70–72)

> (After I heard my teacher call the names
>   of all these knights and ladies of ancient times,
>   pity confused my senses, and I was dazed.)

And with this we have crossed the threshold into the second half of
the canto where the mood is so different from that of the first. There
we were dimly conscious of a nebulous setting of indefinite space,
resounding with the noises of battling winds and with the shrieks,
from far off, of sinners in torment. This dark stage with its unseen
sounds at first was empty, then came to be peopled with a host of
spirits blown through the air, who pass before us, but who are not
described, though we catch some names. But now the winds will
have abated and we shall no longer seem to hear the screams of the
damned, or be conscious of the vast bleak area where we are, for a
spotlight will be suddenly cast on two figures who will come to rest
by the side of the Pilgrim and his guide: out of a welter of forms

and movements, there emerge (as though in bas-relief) the quiet figures of Francesca and Paolo. And for the rest of the canto the action will be staged in the space occupied by these four actors. Finally, the didactic note of the first half of the canto will give way to that of personal revelation; and whereas, there, the voice of Virgil instructing his ward was actually heard only toward the end, here a constant flow of warm words will create an atmosphere of intimacy, in contrast to the impersonal atmosphere of space and dogma which first prevailed.[15]

The second half of the canto begins, however, as if it were a continuation of the first part: just as the Pilgrim in line 50 has shown his interest in the approaching flock of spirits, ("Maestro, chi son quelle/genti . . ."), to be informed of their identity by Virgil, so now he reveals his desire to speak with ". . . quei due che 'nsieme vanno," and is encouraged by Virgil to call them to him. But from now on Virgil will relinquish his role of mentor, leaving the situation entirely in the hands of his pupil; from now on the reader's attention will be centered on Francesca as she tells her story, and on the Pilgrim as he listens, and questions, and listens again.

We hear the Pilgrim's tender appeal[16] and we see two figures gracefully descend from ". . . la schiera ov'è Dido," gliding together toward him with the movement of doves returning to their nest.[17] Francesca will begin and end her first confession, while the Pilgrim, listening, plunged into deep reflection, bows his head; and Virgil, seeing this, elicits from him an account of his thoughts. Turning once more to Francesca, and calling her now by name, the Pilgrim asks a question about her love, which she answers, ending with the line "quel giorno più non vi leggemmo avante." She falls silent, and while Paolo continues to weep, the Pilgrim faints from pity.

In my treatment of the first half of the canto the events were first rapidly summarized so that we could then give our attention to the significance of these events and of the way in which the poet chose to present them—involving the process by which the figure of Virgil, the teacher, comes more and more into focus, the didactic note continuing all the while. Here I have offered a brief summary of the second half of the canto before discussing the deep significance—this time, of a psychological nature—of the encounter between Francesca and the Pilgrim. The light it sheds on the character of Francesca will be discussed in the following chapter; now we shall concentrate on the role played by the Pilgrim, comparing this with the role that his teacher hopefully must have had in mind. For in the first 69 lines of our canto, before Francesca and her silent lover make their appearance on stage, the Pilgrim had been given the chance by Virgil to learn enough to shield himself, when the moment would come, from Francesca's seductiveness. What is it that his teacher intended him to learn?

When he first saw the hideous figure of Minos, the Pilgrim should have realized, with a shock, that he was really in Hell—no longer in Limbo where pity, and even veneration, are not unfitting. He will begin to meet the sinners condemned by Minos, who serves not only the Circle of the Lustful, but all of Hell. And later, when the Pilgrim will meet Francesca he should have remembered Minos, he should have imagined her standing before the monster as he passed judgment on her—with his tail. And her poignant confession of her love might have reminded him that she had confessed the same love, the same sin before the monster—probably with a lesser display of rhetoric and a greater degree of veracity; in fact, her confession to Minos must have begun where her confession to the Pilgrim leaves off: "Quel giorno più non vi leggemmo avante."

When, later, against the background of the screams of the damned and the howling of the winds, Virgil explains the nature of the sin being punished in this circle, and the form of this punishment, perhaps his description of the torments suffered by the sinners arouse a feeling of terrible pity in the young novice. But Virgil has been careful to point out that the loudest screams of these sinners were not just expressions of helpless pain but of hatred for the God who created them. This should not only have tempered the novice's pity, but later, when Francesca would speak so wistfully and deferentially of "the king of the universe," he might have remembered that she belonged to the same blaspheming crew. Also,

Virgil's definition of the sin of lust as the subjection of reason to
desire (reason, the noblest faculty of man—which distinguishes him
from the animals) should have impressed the Pilgrim more deeply
than it evidently did, for when he aches with pity for the elegantly
grieving Francesca, he, too, is subjecting his reason to his feelings.
In this way he is participating in the sin being punished in the
Second Circle.[18]

Again, in Virgil's description of the lustful souls who fly into
the Pilgrim's range of vision, it is the figure of Semiramis, as we
know, that dominates—as horrible in her way as the figure of Minos
at the threshold of the Second Circle. If any personification of lust
should arouse horror in the Pilgrim's soul it is this beautiful, vicious,
and incestuous woman—she is "the *first* among those whom you
ought to know about," said Virgil, before proceeding to name the
less offensive lovers. But the hideousness of her crimes does not
prevent the Pilgrim from reacting with pity over the fate of all
of them.

Finally, Virgil has tried to teach him that, among the damned,
the individual does not count: the damned are a mass in which
individual differences are unimportant blurs. In our canto the souls
of the Lustful first make known their far-away presence (25–30)
by the screams issuing from their countless throats. And in Virgil's
simile of the starlings, it is a picture of their totality that is presented to our imagination: the vaguest of pictures, a shapeless mass
agitated by tumultuous movement. Then (46–69) a more clear-cut
segment of the mass is presented—and presented to view. Virgil
points them out and names them; but what might seem at first an
attempt at individualization, was surely intended to have the opposite effect: more than a thousand names the Pilgrim heard, so
that in the end not a single one could stand out (except, perhaps,
Semiramis). But when Francesca comes on stage with her lover
we soon see how vulnerable the Pilgrim is to her personality, to her
individuality.

It is obvious that he has learned nothing that he should have.
His mood toward Francesca is that of tenderness and compassion

for her fate, and sympathetic association with her feelings—an expansive, one might almost say, self-indulgent pity to which he has subjected his reason. Note his words:

> ... "O anime affannate,
> venite a noi parlar, s'altri nol niega!" (80–81)

> (... "Oh, wearied souls,
> come speak with us if it be not forbidden.")

> ... "Oh lasso,
> quanti dolci pensier, quanto disio
> menò costoro al doloroso passo!" (112–114)

> (... "Alas,
> what sweet thoughts, and oh, how much desiring
> brought these two down into this agony.")

> ... "Francesca, i tuoi martìri
> a lagrimar mi fanno tristo e pio.
> Ma dimmi: al tempo d'i dolci sospiri,
>   a che e come concedette amore
>   che conosceste i dubbiosi disiri?" (116–120)

> (... "Francesca, the torment that you suffer
> brings painful tears of pity to my eyes.
> But tell me, in that time of your sweet sighing
>   how, and by what signs, did love allow you
>   to recognize your dubious desires?")

At the end of the first confession, in which the lovers' fate is presented as having been determined by general laws, we have seen the Pilgrim in a reverie of nostalgic reminiscences; at the end of the second confession, in which Francesca evokes an intimate moment of the lovers' past, he swoons. But, though we can witness the increasing intensity of his pity as he listens to Francesca's words, it is most important to note that he was predisposed to pity the lovers even before they joined him—as is shown by the words opening his invitation: "O anime affannate." Even before his attention had

been drawn to them—just before the second half of the canto
begins—we had seen him wracked with pity (". . . pietà mi giunse
. . ."), pity for the innumerable lustful spirits pointed out to him
by Virgil. The appearance of the word *pietà* in the transitional tercet
sets the tone for the rest of the canto.[19] At the same time, of course,
that it points ahead, it points behind, representing as it does, the
result of Virgil's words to him in the first half of the canto. This
last fact is indeed ironical: Virgil's teachings which had been intended to encourage austerity and impersonality in his pupil's attitude have served only to arouse dazed pity. And the names of the
sinners listed by Virgil which should have inspired a feeling of
moral horror, seem instead to revive in the Pilgrim's memory the
pleasant experiences he had enjoyed while reading the stories of
these famous romantic figures: ". . . le donne antiche e' cavalieri."
(He too, no less than Francesca, shows himself to be the victim of
literature.) This line, showing the transformation, in the Pilgrim's
sentimental imagination, of the damned, blaspheming souls of the
Lustful into *donne antiche e' cavalieri,* makes inevitable the *pietà* of
the line that follows.[20]

I have postponed until the end a discussion of the dove-image
by means of which Francesca and Paolo are brought into focus. We
are first made aware of their presence (and their existence) by the
Pilgrim's request addressed to Virgil which offers the reader a picture of the lovers filtered through the Pilgrim's mind (". . . quei
due che 'nsieme vanno/e paion sì al vento esser leggieri"). Then, in
the following lines (of narrative) we are allowed to see them with
our own eyes—the picture, however, still being colored by the
imagination of the Pilgrim, to whom they appear as two doves
returning to their nest, so instinctively eager must have seemed
their movement toward him, away from "Dido's flock (*la schiera
ov'è Dido*). The beauty of this image is pointed out by most of the
commentators and is surely sensed by every reader, and our appreciation of it is enhanced if we see it in relationship to the two other
bird-images that precede it. That of the starlings offers to our imagination (for we are not allowed to see them) a vivid picture of the

totality of sinners caught up in tumultuous movement; in that of
the cranes, who are presented on stage within our range of vision,
the totality of souls is reduced to that of a single band of sinners
(those of noble or royal lineage, and who were brought to death by
Love), and the movement has subsided to become linear. Finally, in
the image of the doves, the number of the Lustful has been reduced
to two (to an inseparable pair); they are not only within our range
of vision, they are directly before our eyes, caught by the spotlight
which has suddenly illuminated a narrow stage; and the movement
is the diminuendo of a gentle gliding.

But this image is significant not only from the aesthetic point of
view: it also invites to a symbolical interpretation. And if one
thinks of the type of movement on the spiritual plane to which the
flight of doves to their nest could be best compared, surely it would
be the spiritually instinctive ascent of the soul to God whence it
came and where it must return. (Cf. *Psalms* LIV, 6: "Et dixit:
Quis dabit mihi pennas sicut columbae, et volabo, et requiescam?")
And the suggestion in our passage of the harmony of desire (". . .
dal disio chiamate") and will (". . . dal voler portate") could
surely corroborate such an association. It is with a reference to that
same harmony that the *Divine Comedy* will end: "ma già volgeva
il mio disio e 'l velle (sì come rota ch'igualmente è mossa/l'Amor
che move il sole e l'altre stelle)." Yet the Pilgrim applies this image
to two unrepentant sinners in Hell, guilty, as he knows, of screaming
curses against God, who come to him encouraged by his display of
weakness, by his subjection of reason to emotion. Why did the poet
allow the Pilgrim to apply this "Christian metaphor" to these lovers
condemned by God? Was it to suggest a contrast between the
sublime connotations of which this image was capable, and the
trivial use which the Pilgrim made of it, being at this stage unaware
of such connotations, unaccustomed to thinking in terms of the
soul's ascent toward God?[21] And incapable, at this point, of learning
from Virgil, from Reason?

Canto V ends with the Pilgrim's total failure to learn about the
sin of lust—which was intended to be the main action of this canto

(as it is one of the main actions of the *Inferno* to learn about sin as a whole). And this abject failure, the subjection of his reason to sentiment, is symbolized by the Pilgrim's figure, prostrate and unconscious, on the floor of Hell: "e caddi come corpo morto cade."[22]

Surely, the figure of the Pilgrim, prostrate on the ground, undone by pity, that we see in the last line of *Inferno* V must remind us of the protagonist of the *Vita nuova* in one of his many emotional seizures. It is true that the weakness shown by the Pilgrim here is that of excessive pity for another, whereas in the *Vita nuova* it was self-pity that the lover indulged in; but the sentimental uncritical sympathy that the Pilgrim lavished upon Francesca was the same kind of sympathy that the protagonist of the *Vita nuova* had craved for himself.

The *Vita nuova* ends, as everyone believes, with an anticipation of the *Divine Comedy*. By stretching a point or two one could say that the *Divine Comedy* begins with a reminiscence of the *Vita nuova:* that is to say, the *Inferno* begins, the description of the *Inferno* proper begins, with the Pilgrim a prey to the same sickly emotions experienced by the protagonist of the *Vita nuova*.[23]

Paolo and Francesca with Dante and Virgil. Canto V, *Inferno*. From the Vatican, Biblioteca Apostolica, MS Urbino Latino 365. Guglielmo Giraldi and assistants, ca. 1478.

II

Behold Francesca Who Speaks So Well

NOW LET us turn to consider the appealing, tender creature whose words produced in the Pilgrim, already predisposed to compassion, a veritable paroxysm of pity. The majority of scholars who have treated the figure of Francesca have presented her in a highly favorable light. To such an extent is this true, in some cases, that they seem to suggest that the attractiveness of her personality is great enough to atone for her sin.[1]

Since, as I have suggested, they treat her only on the surface, this favorable picture is surely understandable, as is their tone of affection, respect and compassion. For on the surface she is truly one of the most charming creatures to appear (though hers was such a brief appearance) in world literature.

What her words most clearly reveal is the good breeding of the speaker: hers is an aristocratic nature, now fired by ardent memories, now tempered by sweetness and feminine grace. Toward the Pilgrim she shows the quintessence of courtesy and graciousness—as is already revealed in her opening words, "O animal grazioso ..." (88), themselves an echo of the Pilgrim's address to the pair of lovers "O anime affannate ..." (80); indeed, it was surely her gratitude for the Pilgrim's tender greeting that inspired her gracious response. And in the wish suggested by her offer "noi pregheremmo ... della tua pace," her graciousness seems to be inspired by true magnanimity: it is precisely that "peace" which she craves so ardently (and

which is surely reflected in her description of the waters of the river
Po: ". . . dove 'l Po discende / per aver pace . . ."), a peace which
she will never know, that she would like to have assured for the
Pilgrim. And how ready she is to comply with his requests; to his
summons (81), "Venite a noi parlar . . ." she answers,

> "Di quel che udire e che parlar vi piace
>   noi udiremo e parleremo a voi . . ." (49–95)

> ("Whatever pleases you to hear or speak
>   we will hear and we will speak about with you . . .").

And when he asks her to tell him how Paolo and she had allowed
themselves to confess their love to each other (118–120), she ac-
quiesces, even though the telling will cause her pain:

> E quella a me: "Nessun maggior dolore
>   che ricordarsi del tempo felice
>   ne la miseria; e ciò sa 'l tuo dottore.
> Ma s'a conoscer la prima radice
>   del nostro amor tu hai cotanto affetto,
>   dirò come colui che piange e dice . . ." (121–126)

> (And she to me: "There is no greater pain
>   than to remember, in our present grief,
>   past happiness—as well your teacher knows!
> But if your great desire is to learn
>   the very root of such a love as ours,
>   I shall tell you, but in words of flowing tears . . .")

Nor is she sparing with her words—which seem to flow naturally
from her heart.

Her courtesy extends also to Virgil, though he has not addressed
her; on two occasions she shows her awareness of his presence. In
lines 94–95, when she promises to answer the Pilgrim's first request,
she shifts from the *tu* with which she had been addressing him to
the *vi* and *voi* that would include Virgil (remembering, no doubt,
the form of the Pilgrim's request: "Venite a *noi* parlar . . ."); and

before she begins her second confession, she ends her aphorism "Nessun maggior dolore . . ." with a reference to the Pilgrim's "dottore" that she sees before her.[2]

Francesca's aristocratic background is suggested not only by her delicate manners but also by her delicate and often noble language (revealing her familiarity with contemporary literature)—a feature which has impressed most critics, though in describing her style they do little more than point out the "dolce stil nuovo" flavor of her two characterizations of "Love" (100 and 103): "Amor, ch'al cor gentil ratto s'apprende" and "Amor, ch'a nullo amato amar perdona." But her style is not limited to the preciosity of the two lines just mentioned; it reveals a considerable variety of nuances. There is the powerful impact of the entire passage (100–106) beginning with "Amor" and ending ". . . ad una morte," which contains the three-fold description of the (sinister) part played by Love in the development of the feelings between her young kinsman and herself, and in the tragic outcome of their feelings. There is the lofty, yet graceful and tender, tone of the description of her birthplace (97–99): "Siede la terra dove nata fui. . . ." And there is the delicacy, one might even say the femininity, of her words indirectly alluding to the hideous fact of their murder: "noi che *tignemmo* il mondo di *sanguigno*." Not the basic word *sangue* but its derivative *sanguigno* —and the blood which she mentions is a "tint." Finally the poet has even endowed Francesca with a superb mastery of narrative exposition: the story of her fall, opening so casually, so unpretentiously, with the words, "Noi leggiavamo un giorno per diletto . . ." (127), leads up to the passionately dramatic climax (whose inevitability we are made to feel): ". . . la bocca mi basciò tutto tremante." The tension is maintained in the following line with its epigrammatic interpretation of causality: "Galeotto fu 'l libro e chi lo scrisse," then the tension subsides with the calm, haunting, accents of the concluding line (that seems to suggest, delicately, the cessation of all activity): "quel giorno più non vi leggemmo avante."

But the more carefully we study the words of the courteous and cultivated Francesca, the more clearly we become aware of the flaws in her character which she is inadvertently revealing. Her basic weakness is her self-centeredness, and this can be seen even in her gracious attitude toward the Pilgrim. That the caressing words which open her address are inspired by gratitude for his expression of compassion, and for the invitation he extended to the lovers, already suggests, if only slightly, her hunger for appreciation, her pleasure at having been singled out for consideration from among the many others flying there: since the Pilgrim treats Francesca this way, he must be "grazioso e benigno."

The implied wish that follows, "Se fosse amico il re de l'universo,/noi pregheremmo lui de la tua pace" (91–92), was earlier characterized as (perhaps) revealing true magnanimity; but while one cannot deny that her wish springs from a generous impulse, one must also sense a frustrated desire on the part of the aristocratic Francesca to use her influence with the powers that be: with the one of highest rank, "il re de l'universo." Surely, the nobly-born Francesca would delight in the opportunity to intercede with a king for a humble pilgrim.[3] Again, as evidence of her graciousness, I have already mentioned her readiness to comply with the Pilgrim's invitation ("Venite a noi parlar . . ."), her words flowing forth so freely. But surely this flow, this effusiveness is slightly ridiculous: in lines 94–95 the Pilgrim's simple *parlare* has been extended to *parlare* and *udire,* and this pair of verbs is (chiastically) repeated:[4] "Di quel che udire e che parlar vi piace/noi udiremo e parleremo a voi" (94–95). Moreover, while here she gives the Pilgrim *carte blanche* to speak on any theme he may desire—instead of pausing at this point (she has already been speaking for three tercets) to allow him to explain what he had wished to talk about when he called the lovers to him, Francesca flows on with a description of her birthplace. And, as she continues, we are reminded that the Pilgrim had expressed his desire to talk to both of the lovers, and she has just acceded to his request in the same terms,[5] yet neither here nor at any other point in the canto will Paolo be given a chance to speak.[6] In fact, except for her reference to *costui* (101 and 104) and *questi* (135) she appears to completely ignore his presence. She is clearly the dominating member of the pair.

As for the theme with which she chooses to continue her speech, we may note the assured way in which she takes for granted the Pilgrim's interest in such a detail as the location of her birthplace. Could it be that, counting on the widespread circulation of her story, she hopes that this allusion to her birthplace will aid the Pilgrim to identify her (as, indeed, it will)? If so, does this not mean that she would be willing to exploit her own scandal in order to let the Pilgrim realize that he is talking to a well-known person?[7]

The poetic style of the description of her birthplace has already been pointed out, but in spite of the undeniable beauty of the passage, it must make the reader smile. Given the speaker, the lofty tone of the opening lines is incongruous: "Siede la terra dove nata fui/su la marina dove 'l Po discende" (97–98). It could recall the words of Adrian in *Purgatory* XIX, after he has revealed his Papal identity ("scias quod ego fui successor Petri"):

> "Intra Sïestri e Chiaveri s'adima
>   una fiumana bella, e del suo nome
>   lo titol del mio sangue fa sua cima." (100–102)

> ("Between Sestri and Chiavari there pours down
>   a lovely river, and with its name
>   my family decorates its title.")

or Cunizza's elaborate self-identification (*Paradiso* IX, 25–32) in topographical terms, which begins:

> "In quella parte de la terra prava
>   italica che siede tra Rialto
>   e le fontane di Brenta e di Piava,
> si leva un colle, e non surge molt'alto,
>   là onde scese già una facella,
>   che fece a la contrada un grande assalto.

D'una radice nacqui e io ed ella:
  Cunizza fui chiamata, e qui refulgo ... "

("In that part of the depraved land
  of Italy that lies between the Rialto
  and where the Brenta and the Piave have their source,
There rises a hill, and it is not too high,
  from which there once descended a firebrand
  that made a great assault on the surrounding country.
From one same root I and he were born:
  Cunizza I was called, and here I shine ... ")

That Francesca loves to talk, that she knows she talks beautifully and is quite conscious of putting on a performance for the Pilgrim, this should be evident by now (incidentally, Francesca is the only woman allowed to speak in the whole of the *Inferno*). Her histrionic self-consciousness is also borne out by certain expressions in her "second confession"; in her first, she needed three tercets to get started (88–96); now, having warmed up, she still needs two (121–26) before she can really begin. In the two tercets opening with "Nessun maggior dolore ... ." we see a figure plunged into grief by the Pilgrim's question, but heroically forcing herself to comply with his desire, attempting to adopt a philosophical attitude (the sententiousness of ". . . ciò sa 'l tuo dottore"!), only at the end to remind us of the tears she is restraining (". . . come colui che piange e dice").

Up to the present, Francesca has occasionally been grandiloquent or pompous; she has never been pedantic. But her description of Paolo's kiss, "Questi, che mai da me non fia diviso,/la bocca mi basciò tutto tremante," is preceded by a dependent clause, describing Lancelot's kiss, which contains a rare latinate version of the construction *accusativus cum infinitivo:*

"Quando leggemmo *il disïato riso
  esser basciato* da cotanto amante. ..." (133–34)

("It was when we read about those longed-for lips
  now being kissed by such a famous lover. ...")

—literally, "when we read the longed-for lips/to be kissed . . .".
Was her choice of construction due to her desire to display her cul-
ture, the degree to which she had profited by her extensive reading?
Or was it the gentlewoman in her (rather than the blue-stocking)
that chose to describe Lancelot's kiss in such antiseptic terms? In
either case, with this frigid prelude to the account of Paolo's kiss,
itself vibrating with passion, we are offered a most incongruous
juxtaposition.[8]

Now in Francesca's painful words, "Nessun maggior do-
lore . . . ," used to introduce the story of Paolo's kiss, there is obviously contained an appeal to the Pilgrim for his sympathy. This may
remind us of the reason she offers for desiring the Pilgrim's peace:
"poi c'hai pietà del nostro mal perverso"—words that both show her
gratitude for his pity and make a further bid for it by referring to
her punishment as "mal perverso." And this should make us wonder what other indications she gives of her attitude toward the sentence passed upon her; to what extent does she seem to recognize
her guilt, her responsibility for her sin?

Francesca's autobiographical account is unique, for twice she
tells the story of her love, her sin. The first confession she herself
volunteers, reminding us, in this regard, of Guido da Montefeltro,
the only other sinner who takes it upon himself to explain why he is
in Hell; her second confession is an answer to a question from the
Pilgrim who wishes to probe more deeply into the occasion of her
fall. (This is the first and only time the Pilgrim will invite a sinner
to give his own version of how he yielded to temptation.)

In her two-fold account of her love-affair with Paolo, three
movements are indicated: when she and Paolo fell in love; when
they revealed their feelings to each other (while reading the story of
Lancelot); Paolo's kiss. (The fourth stage is only hinted at.) At
each step she presents herself as the victim of an irresistible force:
it was the tyranny of Love that made her reciprocate Paolo's passion,
it was the hypnotic spell of the Old French romance that drew their
eyes together in a mute avowal, it was the quivering lips of Paolo
which brought her to complete surrender.

It is in her description of the first movement—the first movement toward her death—that the irresistibility of the force to which
she yields is stressed the most; whereas the power of the Old French
romance and that of Paolo's kiss happened to find her vulnerable
(as they might not have found another), the power of Love on the
person loved is declared to be such that no one could possibly resist
it: "Amor, ch'a *nullo amato* amar perdona." (In presenting herself
as the victim of an irresistible force she is again like Guido da Montefeltro, and him alone.) And Paolo, too, who began the movement, is
presented as obeying a similarly imperious law: "Amor, ch'al cor
gentil *ratto s'apprende*," a line evoking the idealistic love sung by
Guinizelli and other so-called "dolce stilnovisti."[9]

Thus, according to the two famous lines just quoted, it was not
only inevitable that Paolo fall in love with her and she, therefore,
with him, but the nature of the love that inspired them was beyond
reproach. What, then, are we to think of the words that follow the
Guinizellian reminiscence:

> ["Amor, ch'al cor gentil ratto s'apprende,]
> *prese costui de la bella persona*
> *che mi fu tolta . . ."* (100–102)

> (["Love, that kindles quick in the gentle heart,]
> *seized this one for the beauty of my body,*
> *torn from me . . ."*)

Has Francesca read her poets so carelessly that she can believe that
the love they praise will admit of desire for the lady's "beautiful
body"? The two ideas, the two kinds of love, here juxtaposed, are
mutually exclusive according to the literature she had obviously read.
And it must, of course, be the second of these that represents Paolo's
love as it really was: sensual love (the simple declarative statement
annuls the pretentious relative clause that precedes)—as her love,
too, had to be, since she did respond to his feelings. Perhaps Francesca knew full well the nature of the love "ch'al cor gentil ratto
s'apprende," which should mean that she saw clearly the difference

between that love and the one that brought her to her death. But perhaps she did not see clearly. On the one hand she surely knew that it was the carnal elements of love between her and Paolo that led them to adultery and to Hell; on the other, being a woman, she may have wanted to stress the sweeter, more tender, more exalted aspects of that love and, being well-bred, accustomed to observe the ambiguous code (whereby gentility leads insensibly to hypocrisy) of always showing herself at her best and presenting situations in their most favorable light, she could not face steadily the nature of her sin.[10] And, perhaps, there is also a touch of snobbish poetic aspiration: she must lay claim, somehow, in spite of the evidence, to a love as refined as that treated by the most refined poets.

In the description of the second movement of her love, involving the lovers' revelation to each other of their feelings, even more obvious is the influential role played in their love-affair by literature (in this case a single text), and this is recognized explicitly in Francesca's allusion (137) to the go-between, Galehot, in the Old French romance: "Galeotto fu il libro e chi lo scrisse." But again we must wonder if Francesca was a careless reader, for the event which she is supposedly retelling from the text the lovers read, and which, according to her, inspired Paolo's passionate kiss, never took place in the text in question. As is now well known (and the problem involved has engaged the attention of a number of critics), it was not the timid Lancelot who kissed the "disïato riso" of the queen; it was the sophisticated and coquettish Guinevere who, at the urging of Galehot, decided to kiss the lovesick knight: ". . . et la roine voit que li chevaliers nen ose plus faire, si le prent par le menton e le baise devant Galehot asses longement, si que la Dame de Malohaut seit qu'ele le baise."

It is difficult to believe that Francesca read carelessly the text which made the lovers flush and pale, and drew their eyes together. (And, incidentally, careless reading on her part would imply careless reading on the part of Dante, who is letting her retell the story.) It is also difficult to believe—and with this we now approach the third movement of their love—that a kiss given by Guinevere to

Lancelot would have inspired Paolo to give a kiss to Francesca (un-
less, of course, he too were reading carelessly the passage which
inspired him to adultery). Indeed, it would be more likely that the
Old French text, which they had before their eyes, would have inspired Francesca to follow the queen's example and to kiss Paolo.

And, indeed, I have proposed that the incident of the kiss
between Francesca and Paolo was the reverse of what she describes:
that it was Francesca who took the initiative in the lovemaking.[11]
If this is true, it is now understandable why she also inverted the
roles played by Lancelot and Guinevere: since she had made the Old
French romance responsible for their kiss, and since she wished to
present Paolo as taking the first step in the expression of their guilty
love, she had to present the Lancelot of the romance as taking the
first step. Two false versions, the first one that she gives (that
Lancelot kissed the queen) made necessary by the ensuing one that
she plans to give (that Paolo kissed her). Must we then think of
Francesca as a calculating person who knowingly tells a double lie
in order to put the blame on her lover for what she herself has done
—two lies in order to betray?

I think one cannot use the word "calculating" and "knowingly"
of Francesca and her misrepresentation (though, in my earlier article, I was somewhat more harsh toward her). If we remember the
confusion that she showed in her first confession, how her hypo-
critical suggestion of the purity of their love is immediately contra-
dicted in the next line by her own reference to her beautiful body—it
is difficult to attribute to her, in her second confession, such a degree
of mental clarity as could enable her to foresee the necessity of
planting one lie in order to make a second one credible. Perhaps,
here, too, we have to do with mental confusion, which must also
imply moral confusion. Perhaps Francesca, like so many persons
concerned with their own prestige, has developed the ability to
remember past events in a way that redounds to her credit. It would
have been only "normal" if Paolo had been the one to give the first
kiss, and so her memory conveniently allows her to believe that this

is what happened. She has "forgotten" that it was she who kissed first, inspired by the text they were reading—consequently she must "forget" that in that text it was Guinevere who kissed Lancelot. The image of the self-assured queen who took the timid Lancelot by the chin and kissed him "longuement" had faded in her memory, replaced by a gentle figure of sweet compliancy such as she now "remembers" herself to have been.[12]

So far we have presented Francesca's story of her love with its three movements as if it were a continuous flow from the first to the second to the third. Actually, of course, there is a sharp break after her first confession, ending line 106, which contains a description of the initial stage of her love and a sudden reference to the death of the two lovers. In this confession the second and third stage are not mentioned; we are told only about the birth of Love and, suddenly, about death. And Francesca surely believed that with her depiction of the efficacy of love:

> "Amor, ch'al cor gentil ratto s'apprende
> . . . .
> Amor, ch'a nullo amato amar perdona
> . . . .
> Amor condusse noi ad una morte."

her story is told. But the Pilgrim (moved to tender compassion by her words, and perhaps puzzled by her implication that such a sweet love could lead to sin and death) asks her a question (118–120): how did it come about that love allowed them to recognize their dubious desires and reveal them to each other? (He asks her to tell him about the second stage.) Francesca will answer this question by telling about the day when she and Paolo read the love story of Lancelot, which moved them so deeply—ending with a delicate allusion to the third stage (sensuous indulgence) about which the Pilgrim had not inquired.

But the words that introduce her second account are curious indeed, and they seem to reveal another example of confusion or disingenuousness on her part. Francesca agrees to tell the Pilgrim, since he so desires, about "the first root" of their love:

> "Ma s'a conoscer la prima radice
>   del nostro amor tu hai cotanto affetto,
>   dirò . . ." (124–126)

> ("But if your great desire is to learn
>   the very root of such a love as ours,
>   ˙I shall tell you . . .")

But this is not what the Pilgrim had inquired about (in fact, Francesca had already described "the first root" in her description of love); he is urging her to tell him how the first tender stirrings then *took shape,* how the unavowed longings were allowed to reveal themselves—which is, in fact, what Francesca proceeds to do in her reference to the Old French prose romance. Why then does she preface her account of the reading of the book with a reference to "la prima radice"? Is she trying to pretend that their reading to-gether represented the very beginning, "the root" of their love; that, if it had not been for the text of *Lancelot del Lac,* they would never have fallen in love? This, of course, would be in flagrant contradic-tion to her first analysis of causality: the love ". . . ch' al cor gentil ratto s'apprende" needs no book.[13] The total confusion manifest in Francesca's attempts to remember, and to explain—a confusion mainly caused by her determination to see herself, and to present herself, in as favorable a light as possible—this has been sensed by none of the critics I have read.[14] In fact, Foscolo was able to speak of the ". . . truthfulness [which] beautifies her confession of desire" and Renato Poggioli says that she "has given proof of intellectual and moral courage by facing truth in all its nakedness . . ." (p.339).

We have already seen that Francesca in her two confessions takes every means possible to excuse her sin by presenting it as caused by forces beyond her control, and of course we could not possibly have expected to find in her words any indication of repentance: it is the law of Hell that the sinner, once damned for his failure to repent on earth, is not given a second chance to repent. But, in addition to a total lack of repentance, do we also find any indications of defiance against Divine Justice (if so, we must expect them to be implicit rather than explicit)? Many scholars believe to have found them, insofar as they read into Francesca's words a fierce loyalty to her lover, to her love, to her sin. They speak in terms of an undying love which has triumphed over death and over Hell, a love in which she glories. Perhaps Grandgent may be quoted briefly as one of the more sober exponents of that theory: "Amid the tortures of Hell, where all is hatred, her love does not forsake her, and she glories in the thought that she and Paolo shall never be parted."[15]

The two passages that have inspired these words of Grandgent, and on which others, too, have based their opinion, are the following:

> "Amor. . .
>   mi prese del costui piacer sì forte
>   *che, come vedi, ancor non m'abbandona."* (103–105)

> ("Love. . .
>   seized me so strongly with delight in him
>   that, as you see, he never leaves my side.")

and

> "Quando leggemmo . . . ,
>   . . . .
>   questi, *che mai da me non fia diviso*
>   la bocca mi basciò. . . ." (133–136)

> (". . . when we read . . . ,
>   . . . .
>   . . . this one, who shall never leave my side,
>   then kissed my mouth. . . .")

On the surface the words italicized in each passage may seem to justify the interpretation suggested above: happy, triumphant insistence on the inseparability of the two lovers. But such a "triumph over Hell" would contradict the principles of divine punitive justice as these are reflected throughout the *Inferno*. How can we believe that the poet would make an exception of Paolo and Francesca, whom he presents (as a lesson to the Pilgrim) as the first sinners he encounters in Hell?

But there are other reasons against this romantic amoral interpretation. In the first place eternal togetherness in itself is not necessarily a cause for exultation, it may also be the cause of deepest anguish (one may think of Sartre's *Huis clos*). We must see Francesca's words as ambiguous, and I prefer to take them in the second, more tragic sense. We cannot, of course, imagine that their constant companionship represents a choice on the part of the two lovers, the indulgence of a mutual desire. No, if they go always together it must be because they are forced to do so (together in Hell because they were slain together in their sin). And how could it make Francesca happy—or, rather, how could it alleviate her suffering— to know herself never to be free of the naked body of her dead lover, this constant reminder of passion spent, of the sin that condemned them, of shameful exposure and death? Rather, their inseparability could well be the bitterest aspect of their punishment. And the silent, weeping figure of Paolo certainly does not suggest one who is glorying in his love.[16]

Nor during the scene where Francesca holds the center of the stage does she give the slightest indication of enjoying the presence of her lover. We have already seen how Paolo is immediately eclipsed as soon as she begins to speak. She never turns to him, even for a brief moment, to address him. As has already been said, if it were not for the *costui* and the *questi* with which she reminds us of his presence, we could easily forget that he is on stage (until she finishes speaking, and we learn that Paolo has been weeping all the while). She does not call him by his name or by any endearing term (and, of course, there is no *tu*); she merely points to a near-by figure: *costui, questi*. These two deictic, distantiating pronouns evoke a minimum of humanity, of individuality.

As we listen to Francesca's words, with their adverbial reminders of eternity: ". . . che . . *ancor* non mi abbandona." and
". . . che *mai* da me non fia diviso," referring to the figure who
will always be by her side, we must hear in her words bitterness,
hopelessness, dull anguish, terrible resignation.

In fact, I am so convinced that Francesca loathes Paolo's presence that I should like to offer a new interpretation of the much-
debated line 102: ". . . e 'l modo ancor m'offende." I agree with
those who see in *modo* a reference to the manner of the lovers'
death and, more specifically, with those who see, in the "offense"
mentioned, the exposure of the lovers in their intimacy.[17] But there
may well be an additional element in this "offense": not only were
they exposed together, they were killed together. For this reason,
they must remain together forever in Hell, and I believe it is this
that "offends" Francesca more than the temporary exposure of the
lovers in their intimacy. Note that the *ancor* of line 102 is paralleled
by the *ancor* that follows three lines later which, in turn, points
toward the *mai* of line 135:

   ". . . la bella persona
che mi fu tolta; e 'l modo *ancor* m'offende." (101–102)

   ". . . come vedi, *ancor* non m'abbandona." (105)

"questi, che *mai* da me non fia diviso,
   la bocca mi basciò. . . ." (135–36)

Thus, her two references to their fated inseparability are stylistically
linked with the reference to the manner of their death ("e 'l
modo . . ."). The "manner" of their death "still" torments her, for
she is "still" linked with Paolo who will "never" leave her.

Thus Francesca's words themselves spell out her doom. For a
brief moment, with the Pilgrim, she could perform, she could pretend, she could be the gracious lady she had been in the beautiful
life on earth. But when the Pilgrim, with his "doctor" will have

taken his leave, she will be left alone with her silent lover Paolo, in Hell, forever.

☙ ❧

In the preceding chapter we left the Pilgrim prostrate and un-conscious on the floor of Hell, symbolizing the subjection of his reason to sentiment, and now we have seen the figure of Francesca, so appealing on the surface and, within, so vain, so confused, and ultimately so treacherous to her lover, who stirred the Pilgrim to such overwhelming compassion. This is the figure, condemned to Hell for having indulged in adulterous, incestuous lust (of which she is totally unrepentant), who has caused the Pilgrim to fail so ignominiously his test. For surely his encounter with Francesca was intended as a test—a test of his ability to see Francesca's sin for what it was.

Now, granted that I am right about the falsity that I see re-vealed in Francesca's words, one might object that the Pilgrim in his brief encounter with her, dazed and shaken as he had to be by his recent experiences, could hardly be expected to take in the vari-ous levels of Francesca's *vanitas*. But it was not for vanity, or empti-ness, or phoniness, or any other flaw in her personality that Francesca was condemned to Hell; she was condemned to the Second Circle for her lust. And that she was lustful the Pilgrim did know. It is not because he failed to analyze her personality with more acumen that he is tacitly condemned by the author of the *Divine Comedy;* it is because he reacted to her personality, he reacted to Francesca as to an individual lady, with a name of her own, such as might be encoun-tered in society (or in romantic literature)—and not to the incarna-tion of lust unrepented. Instead of allowing her charm to mitigate her sinfulness, the Pilgrim should have seen her sinfulness against the background of her arrant lack of penitence—as revealed so clearly in her words.

I have said that Francesca is the only woman in the *Inferno* al-lowed to speak; and she is the first speaker in Hell, the first sinner. In the role she plays with Paolo, this "first sinner" must remind us of the first human being to sin in Christian history. Is not Francesca Eve? And not content with having seduced Paolo in the flesh, this *figura Evae* has attempted successfully to seduce the Pilgrim, who is Everyman, into committing not the sin of lust itself but what has been defined as the essence of Lust: the subjection of reason to emotion. And this is precisely what the original Eve did to Adam, the father of Everyman. In fact, the abstract formula offered by Virgil defines not only the essence of lust but also the essence of sin itself— which first came into the world through Eve.

Canto V of the *Inferno* that introduces us to the realm of the damned in Hell is the only one in which Dante the Poet allows the Pilgrim to be tempted by a sinner. His *descensus ad infernum* had to begin with his total surrender to temptation.

Dante and Virgil observe Phlegyas approaching; in the distance—the tower with two lights. Canto VIII, *Inferno*. From the Vatican, Biblioteca Apostolica, MS Latino 4776. Florentine, ca. 1390-1400.

III

From Measurement to Meaning: Simony

I N CANTO XIX of the Inferno the Pilgrim learns about the punishment meted out to the simonists, whose torment consists of being buried head down, in various deep openings in the ground, one on top of the other, the protruding feet of the one on top being licked by oily flames. The main part of this canto is devoted to a dialogue between the Pilgrim and one of the most nefarious of the simonists, Nicholas III, who, as we soon learn, expects to be joined in the course of time by two other simonists still more infamous, Boniface VIII and Clement V.

The main didactic purpose of this canto is to reveal the horror of the sin of simony, the exploitation of ecclesiastical office for private gain; and this canto distinguishes itself from all the other thirty-three in the *Inferno* in the intensity of moral anger it reveals. For the first time, Dante the Pilgrim confronts a sinner with the enormity of his guilt. Many commentators have noted the special fervor of the didactic passages in Canto XIX,[1] but few have attempted to show, in detail, how the moral lesson learned (and taught) by the Pilgrim in this canto has been set in relief by the artistry of its structure. This will be the main purpose of the present chapter, and it will necessitate a step-by-step analysis of the text.

The first two tercets, which consist of an invective against the simonists, are followed almost immediately by an apostrophe to Divine Justice. Then three tercets (13–21) describing the place where the sinners are confined are followed by three more (22–30) that describe the victims themselves. In the next five tercets (31–45) the Pilgrim, having questioned Virgil as to the identity of one of the victims who has attracted his attention, is transported by his guide to the abode of this particular spirit. In lines 46–57 the Pilgrim addresses Nicholas III, who answers him with the question that begins: "Is it you, Boniface?"—a question which so stuns Virgil's ward that he must consult with his guide, who simply advises him to reply in the negative (58–63). In lines 64–87 Nicolas offers a brief autobiographical sketch with certain prophetical details, and the Pilgrim's caustic response occupies lines 90–117. The next two tercets (118–123) describe the anger of Nicolas, and Virgil's satisfaction. The canto ends (123–133) with the Pilgrim, again in the arms of his guide, being returned to the bridge and deposited at the mid-point of the next bolgia.

Already in the opening lines Dante's horror of the sin of simony is most effectively expressed: this canto begins not with narrative or description but with an apostrophe in which we hear the voice of Dante the Poet inveighing against Simon Magus and his followers:

> O Simon Mago, o miseri seguaci
>   che le cose di Dio, che di bontate
>   deon essere spose, e voi rapaci
> per oro e per argento avolterate,
>   or convien che per voi suoni la tromba,
>   però che ne la terza bolgia state. (1–6)
>
> (O Simon Magus! O scum that followed him!
>   Those things of God that rightly should be wed
>   to holiness, you, rapacious creatures,
> for the price of gold and silver, prostitute.
>   Now, in your honor, I must sound my trumpet
>   here in the third bolgia where you are packed.)

In addition to the emotional force of the outburst, two other factors contribute to its extraordinary dramatic impact. First, it has no apparent connection with the end of the preceding canto (Virgil's casual words about Thaïs, in the closing line of Canto XVIII, are immediately followed by Dante's invective: "O Simon Mago"). Secondly, this apostrophe anticipates unexpectedly the sequence of events in the narrative: at this point Dante the Pilgrim, who does not yet know the nature of the sin being punished in the third bolgia, could not possibly have thought in terms of the originator of this sin. Anyone who reads this for the fiirst time (or any scholar capable of reliving his first, naive, fresh impression)[2] must be stunned by the sudden cry "O Simon Mago" that opens the canto; he must be shocked into reading with greater emotional awareness.[3]

Nor is Dante content with this single instance of shock effect: after the six-line apostrophe, the narrative quietly begins anew, establishing continuity with the preceding canto:

> Già eravamo, a la seguente tomba,
>   montati de lo scoglio in quella parte
>   ch'a punto sovra mezzo 'l fosso piomba. (7–9)

> (We had already climbed to see this tomb,
>   and were standing high above it on the bridge,
>   exactly at the mid-point of the ditch.)

only to be interrupted by a second outburst in which Dante, again speaking with foreknowledge, anticipates the justice to be meted out to the sinners mentioned at the start:

> O somma sapïenza, quanta è l'arte
>   che mostri in cielo, in terra e nel mal mondo,
>   e quanto giusto tua virtù comparte! (10–12)

> (O Highest Wisdom, how you demonstrate
>   your art in Heaven, on earth, and here in Hell!
>   How justly does your power make awards!)

How effectively this second interruption, no less unexpected than the first, suggests the intensity of Dante's moral indignation: the uncontrollable intensity that, having temporarily abated, must burst forth anew at the expense of narrative continuity! And with this twice-repeated dramatic device revealing such passionate personal conviction, Dante the poet has, at the beginning, set the tone that Dante the Pilgrim (as we shall see later on) will learn to echo before the canto ends.[4] We shall also see how these two instances of "interruption of the narrative" fit into the movement of the first half of the canto, whose narrative flow obeys the rhythm of postponement.

Canto XVIII having ended with a description of the whore Thäis in the second bolgia, the narrative part of our canto begins with the Pilgrim and Virgil passing over the third. They have, in fact, reached precisely the mid-point of the arch traversing the bolgia: note in line 9 the "punto sovra mezzo," the first of a series of careful specifications of measurement. If the opening narrative tercet (7–9) serves to locate the travelers in space, the second one describes the topography of the third bolgia spread out beneath the gaze of the Pilgrim standing at the mid-point of the arch: he sees a landscape of "livid-colored rock" perforated by holes all of the same circumference, and all perfectly round. And they match exactly those in the Baptistry of San Giovanni in Florence:

> Io vidi per le coste e per lo fondo
>> piena la pietra livida di fóri,
>> d'un largo tutti e ciascun era tondo.
> Non mi parean men ampi né maggiori
>> che que' che son nel mio bel San Giovanni,
>> fatti per loco d'i battezzatori. (13–18)

> (I saw along the sides and on the bottom
>> the livid-colored rock all full of holes;
>> all were the same in size, and each was round.
> To me they seemed no wider and no deeper
>> than those inside my lovely San Giovanni
>> made for priests to stand in or baptize from.)

With this comparison the narrative flow again has been arrested, nor is it immediately resumed. Dante continues his digression with another tercet which includes an autobiographical reminiscence: his breaking of a baptismal font (or stall)[5] in San Giovanni in order to rescue a victim trapped within—

> l'un de li quali, ancor non è molt' anni
>   rupp' io per un che dentro v'annegava:
>   e questo sia suggel ch'ogn' omo sganni! (19–21)

> (And one of these, not many years ago,
>   I smashed for someone who was drowning in it:
>   let this be mankind's picture of the truth!)

The six lines 16-21 (just as was true of the two six-line apostrophes), could be neatly removed from the canto without the slightest detriment to the narrative: line 15 ("all were the same in size, and each was round") would flow immediately into line 22 ("from the mouth of every hole were sticking out . . .").

What is the effect of this new interruption, this casual, almost rambling digression, so different in tone from the first two vehement outbursts? Many commentators have treated in great detail the passage in question, but only Spitzer[6] has sensed that it was poetically motivated; according to him the allusion to San Giovanni, evocative to any Florentine reader, was introduced in order to aid us in visualizing in its minutest details the locality that he is describing. This careful simile, in turn, leads directly, easily, to the reminiscence ". . . And one of these, not many years ago"—a statement which serves to fix the scene in time as well as space, and which, because of its personal flavor and also because of its authenticity (an event that actually happened on this earth to Dante the man), serves by association to endow an other-worldly scene with the "reality" of experiences in this life—a constant aim of Dante the poet. I shall come back to this autobiographical digression, and in particular to line 21, to discuss at greater length its function in the canto.

If we accept this as the only purpose of the digression represented by lines 16-21, Dante would have interrupted the narrative to add vividness and convincingness to his description, just as twice before he had done so in order to impress the reader with the force of his moral passion (though Spitzer has nothing to say of the two previous interruptions). But this digression, unlike the first two, would have been effective regardless of its contents; this interruption is also effective *qua* interruption, for it serves to present to us gradually, by stages, what the Pilgrim must have seen at a glance as he looked down from his vantage point over the exact center of the bolgia. The reader thinks that in lines 13-15 he has been told everything the Pilgrim had seen: an uninhabited expanse of rock perforated with many neat holes, all the same size, perfectly round. Only now, after having evoked the Baptistry in Florence, after having told us of the part he once played there, only now does Dante tell us that there is something in the holes:

> Fuor de la bocca a ciascun soperchiava
> d'un peccator li piedi e de le gambe
> infino al grosso, e l'altro dentro stava.
> Le piante erano a tutti accese intrambe;
> per che sì forte guizzavan le giunte,
> che spezzate averien ritorte e strambe.
> Qual suole il fiammeggiar de le cose unte
> muoversi pur su per la strema buccia,
> tal era lì dai calcagni a le punte.   (22–30)

> (From the mouth of every hole were sticking out
> a single sinner's feet, and then the legs
> up to the calf—the rest was stuffed inside.
> The soles of every sinner's feet were flaming;
> their naked legs were twitching frenziedly—
> they would have broken any chain or rope.
> Just as a flame will only move along
> an object's oily outer peel, so here
> the fire slid from heel to toe and back.)

What they contain are human bodies; what we are finally allowed to see is a collection of legs and feet. And these legs emerging from the holes are presented as though they were so many additional features of topography, their proportions measured off with the same precision that we have had occasion to note twice before in reference to the measurement of inanimate objects: of each pair of legs we see only the part below the calf (*infino al grosso:* 24). There is no doubt that in these three tercets there is a dehumanizing, even de-animizing principle at work in the description of the sinners' bodies (that is, of the visible parts of their bodies). The soles of the feet are licked by flames as if they were merely disconnected objects burning; indeed, in line 28 there is a comparison with things, oily things ("cose unte"): the flames glide as they would over an oily surface,[7] their movement limited between the heel and the toe of the foot (30: "dai calcagni alle punte").[8] Only in this last tercet do we see what must have first caught the Pilgrim's attention when he looked down: the array of paired-off flames waving like so many pairs of torches. And even now, though the description has come to an end, we have still to learn one other all-important detail: that there was a particular pair of legs that distinguished itself from the others by waving more wildly and burning more brightly. Instead of presenting this picture directly to our sight, Dante, after finishing his description of the circle, will have his Pilgrim turn to Virgil to inquire:

> "Chi è colui, maestro, che si cruccia
>   guizzando più che gli altri suoi consorti,"
>   diss' io, "e cui più roggia fiamma succia?" (31–33)

> ("Who is that one, Master, that angry wretch,
>   who is writhing more than any of his comrades,"
>   I asked, "the one licked by a redder flame?")

Again the reader is made to realize that a part of the picture had been withheld from him.

But the Pilgrim's question is interesting also because of the type of curiosity it reveals: instead of inquiring about the nature of the sin being punished in this bolgia (of which he is still ignorant), he simply asks Virgil to identify this particular sinner. Why does he wish to know the name of one out of a number of fellow sinners? Actually the Pilgrim seems to be offering us the motive for his

curiosity: this particular pair of legs happened to be the most conspicuous. Absorbed in the contemplation of a moving, shining
object he is completely oblivious to the problems of crime and punishment that he had come to Hell to investigate!

The question, "Che è colui . . . ?" Virgil does not answer, suggesting instead that his ward learn from the sinner himself, to whom
he will transport him. The two tercets concerning Virgil's offer and
the Pilgrim's acceptance contain a most curious dialogue (a dialogue, incidentally, which also serves the purpose of postponement).
The Pilgrim has asked "Che è colui . . . ?" to be answered by Virgil:

> Ed elli a me: "Se tu vuo' ch'i' ti porti
>   là giù per quella ripa che più giace,
>   da lui saprai di sé e de' suoi torti." (34–36)

> (And he to me, "If you want to be carried down
>   along that lower bank to where he is,
>   you can ask him who he is and why he's here.")

But, obviously, the Pilgrim has said nothing of any desire to descend.
Is Virgil attempting to put words into the Pilgrim's mouth—or has
he sensed his unspoken desire? The first two and a half lines of the
Pilgrim's response:

> E io: "Tanto m'è bel, quanto a te piace:
>   tu se' signore, e sai ch'i' non mi parto
>   dal tuo volere, e sai quel che si tace." (37–39)

> (And I, "My pleasure is what pleases you:
>   you are my lord, you know that from your will
>   I would not swerve. You even know my thoughts.")

would seem to imply the former (the Pilgrim would have realized
from Virgil's suggestion that his leader is in favor of the idea). The
last half of the third line, however, suggests the latter possibility:
"you even know my thoughts." I think that this last part of the

tercet should determine the interpretation of the whole response, particularly since there are frequent mentions in the *Commedia* of Virgil's ability to read his disciple's mind. The Pilgrim, then, would be saying (in reverse) : yes, the impulse to speak with that one below did come to me and, now that I know that you approve it, can say "My pleasure is what pleases you." The elaborate courtesy of the Pilgrim's reply, often noted by the commentators, no doubt reflects his great relief at discovering that his secret desire met with his guide's approval. And his courteous words are then matched by the tender solicitude of Virgil, who insists on carrying his charge all the way down, right to the edge of the hole containing the anguished legs (line 45) "of that one who was fretting with his shanks":

> Allor venimmo in su l'argine quarto;
>   volgemmo e discendemmo a mano stanca
>   là giù nel fondo foracchiato e arto.
> Lo buon maestro ancor de la sua anca
>   non mi dipuose, sì mi giunse al rotto
>   di quel che sì piangeva con la zanca. (40–45)

> (When we reached the fourth bank, we began to turn
>   and, keeping to the left, made our way down
>   to the bottom of the holed and narrow ditch.
> The good guide did not drop me from his side
>   until he brought me to the broken rock
>   of that one who was fretting with his shanks.)

(Note the contemptuous tone of the vulgar word *zanca*, matched, incidentally, by the equally pejorative *piote* in line 120, which suggests "big flat feet.")

Now the reader had surely expected that the question, "Chi è colui . . . ?" would be answered immediately by Virgil (as was usually the case thus far in the *Inferno*); instead, he has had to wait during the exchange of courtesies, and he must wait while the journey downward is so carefully described, expecting all the while (waiting in suspense) to hear the answer from the sinner himself.

But when the moment comes, the Pilgrim does not even put the question to him:

> "O qual che se' che 'l di sù tien di sotto,
>   anima trista come pal commessa,"
> comincia' io a dir, "se puoi, fa motto." (46–48)

> ("O whatever you are, holding your upside down,
>   wretched soul, stuck in the ground like a stake,
>   make some sound," I said, "that is, if you can.")

He does not ask "Who are you?" (he seems indifferent to the question of identity) but only says "Make some sound, that is, if you can." Although there is no description of the feelings of the Pilgrim as he sees before his eyes the pair of writhing, burning legs jutting from the hole, his words of address surely suggest horror and perplexity: is he looking at something human? (Note the ambiguity of the words *qual che se'* "whatever you are.") Before asking for information, then, the Pilgrim must reassure himself that this object before him has the power of speech. And so he only asks, "se puoi, fa motto."

The commentators do not seem to have noted the linguistic innovation achieved in this line by the poet, who, for one moment, has made his language do what it cannot do. Every language has phrases, mainly of a popular flavor, which are used only in the negative: "he didn't say a word, he didn't say beans, there wasn't a peep out of him, he didn't bat an eyelash, he didn't move a muscle." One can hardly imagine: "he said beans," or "he batted an eyelash," or even "he said a word" (period). Professor Hatcher has called to my attention the great likelihood that "fare motto" is one of these expressions (cf **XXXIV**, 66: "Vedi come si storce, e non fa motto"), and my subsequent investigation has turned up not a single example of an affirmative "fare motto."[9] What Dante, then, would have done is to extract from the common expression "non far motto" that minimal element "motto," which is normally posited only in order to be denied, as representing the most he could expect in the way of human speech from the pair of legs before him.

We wait for the result as the Pilgrim bends over the sinner in the attitude of a priest hearing the last confession of a condemned criminal:

> Io stava come 'l frate che confessa
> lo perfido assessin, che, poi ch'è fitto
> richiama lui per che la morte cessa. (49–51)

> (I stood there like a priest hearing confession
> from a vile assassin who, once fixed in his ditch,
> calls him back again to put off dying.)

From within the hole comes a yell:

> Ed el gridò: "Se' tu già costì ritto?
> se' tu già costì ritto, Bonifazio?
> Di parecchi anni mi mentì lo scritto.
> Se' tu sì tosto di quell'aver sazio
> per lo qual non temesti tòrre a 'nganno
> la bella donna, e poi di farne strazio?" (52–57)

> (He cried: "Is that you, here, already, upright?
> Is that you here already upright, Boniface?
> By many years the book has lied to me!
> Are you fed up so soon with all that wealth
> for which you did not fear to take by guile
> the beautiful lady, then tear her asunder?")

Now, who is the more amazed? Nicolas, who, waiting for years to hear the voice of Boniface VIII (who would come, and who must be the next one to come, on a date he foresaw, to join him in his punishment, pushing him farther down into the hole), suddenly, some years too soon, hears the voice of one standing upright?[10] Or the Pilgrim, who had merely asked, by the way of experiment: "se puoi, fa motto," and who, as a result, finds himself mistaken for Boniface: "Se' tu già costì ritto,/se' tu già costì ritto, Bonifazio?"[11] Surely our Pilgrim is the more amazed:

> Tal mi fec' io quai son color che stanno,
> per non intender ciò ch'è lor risposto,
> quasi scornati, e risponder non sanno. (58–60)

> (I stood there like a person just made fun of,
> dumbfounded by a question for an answer,
> not knowing how to answer the reply.)

He is so taken aback that he stands there dumb. Virgil must prompt him:

> Allor Virgilio disse: "Dilli tosto:
> 'Non son colui, non son colui che credi'."
> E io rispuosi come a me fu imposto. (61–63)

> (Then Virgil said: "Quick, hurry up and tell him:
> 'I'm not the one, I'm not the one you think!' "
> And I answered just the way he told me to.)

(Does Virgil repeat "I'm not the one" because of Nicolas' twice repeated question: "Se' tu già costì ritto,/se' tu già costì ritto, Bonifazio?") Meekly, like a schoolboy, his ward obeys; the words "e io rispuosi come a me fu imposto," surely mean that he said: "Non son colui, non son colui che credi." To Nicolas' ears buried in the ground must have come four times the words: "Non son colui. . . ." The disappointed Nicolas kicks his legs in vexation, and sighing and in a whining voice asks him a question—only to continue speaking before the Pilgrim is able to answer:

> Per che lo spirto tutti storse i piedi;
> poi, sospirando e con voce di pianto,
> mi disse: "Dunque che a me richiedi?
> Se di saper ch'i' sia ti cal cotanto
> che tu abbi però la ripa corsa,
> sappi chi'i' fui vestito del gran manto. . . ." (64–69)

> (The spirit heard, and twisted both his feet,
> then, sighing with a grieving, tearful voice
> he said: "Well then, what do you want of me?
> If it concerns you so to learn my name
> that for this reason you came down the bank,
> know that I once was dressed in the great mantle. . . .")

This fact should not surprise us at this point: our Pilgrim's intended question "Who are you?" will never get asked in the canto (nor will it ever be directly answered).

Surely there is humor in the whole passage from 46 ("O qual che se' che 'l di sù tien di sotto") to 66 ("mi disse: 'Dunque che a me richiedi?' "); there is described a most amusing comedy of errors.[12] Indeed, perhaps the humor spills over beyond line 66 into the space between 66 and 67 or into the next two lines, for it must be noted that the question in 66 is not answered by the Pilgrim. Should we imagine that he has still not recovered from the shock of being mistaken for Boniface VIII? In this case we must imagine, after "Dunque che a me richiedi?" a pause filled with the silence of the dumbfounded Pilgrim—and only after receiving no reply would Nicolas, in order to allow the Pilgrim more time to recover, offer himself (67–68) the probable explanation for the latter's presence: "If it concerns you so to learn my name/that for this reason you came down the bank . . ." (Note that this indirect question concerning Nicolas' identity—the question which is never directly answered—occurs in the exact middle of the canto.) In that case, the humor, as I have suggested, would consist in Dante's silence: the space between lines 66–67. Or are we to imagine an unbroken sequence of words? This would mean that Nicolas was the garrulous type that never gives his interlocutor a chance to answer the question asked. In this case the humor would reside in Nicolas' words continuing into 67–68: the narrow central section that serves as the hinge for the two (so dissimilar) halves of our canto. In either case, the Pilgrim has missed the chance to ask the question which from the start he wished to have answered; in either case, whether we imagine the Pilgrim as tongue-tied, unable to answer a very simple question, or as about to speak only to have the words promptly taken out of his mouth, he does offer a slightly ridiculous picture of impotence.

Already in the first line of the second half of the canto (69) there is a change of tone; there is a proud ring to the words: "sappi ch' i' fui vestito del gran manto." This line, describing Nicolas' former lofty status as Head of the Church, must also suggest the picture of his person, once clothed in dignity, now showing us his writhing naked legs. It is as if, with these words, Nicolas were attempting to cover his exposed limbs as well as to evoke the great dignity of his office. This opening line, in a general way, sets the mood for the second half of the canto, where the tone, at times harsh and bitter, at times calm and gentle, is always of a high seriousness.

The rest of Nicolas' speech, which ends at line 87, can be quickly summarized because of its simple, well-organized structure. In lines 70–72 he succinctly states the nature of his crime and of his punishment, ending with the famous epigrammatic representation of his contrappasso:

> "E veramente fui figliuol de l'orsa,
>   cupido sì per avanzar li orsatti,
>   che sù l'avere e qui me misi in borsa." (70–72)

> ("But actually I was the she-bear's son,
>   so greedy to advance my cubs, that wealth
>   I pocketed in life, and here, myself.")

All the rest of Nicolas' speech has to do with his companions in sin. He first tells of those who had preceded him in this world, in sin and in suffering (73–75); he next (76–78) speaks of one who will come after him—in the next world, at the same time that he offers a courteous explanation for having mistaken the Pilgrim's identity and having questioned him so abruptly:

> "Di sotto al capo mio son li altri tratti,
>   che precedetter me simoneggiando,
>   per le fessure de la pietra piatti.
> Là giù cascherò io altresì, quando
>   verrà colui ch'i' credea che tu fossi,
>   allor ch'i' feci 'l sùbito dimando." (73–78)

("Beneath my head are pushed down all the others
   who came, sinning in simony, before me,
   squeezed tightly in the fissures of the rock.
I, in my turn, shall join the rest below
   as soon as he comes, the one I thought you were
   when, all too quick, I put my question to you.")

In the following lines, the duration of his present position in the
hole is compared with that of Boniface's expected stay in the same
position—the comparison being expressed in terms of physical
torment:

"Ma più è 'l tempo già che i piè mi cossi
   e ch'i' son stato così sottosopra,
   ch'el non starà piantato coi piè rossi. . . ."   (79–81)

("But already my feet have baked a longer time
   and I have been stuck upside-down like this
   than he will stay here planted with feet aflame. . . .")

This tercet serves as a prelude to the two final ones, which describe,
in terms of his sinfulness, the third of the triad of papal sinners
singled out for excoriation in this canto, who will come, in time, to
take his place in Hell:

"Ché dopo lui verrà, di più laida opra,
   di ver' ponente, un pastor sanza legge,
   tal che convien che lui e me ricuopra.
Nuovo Iasón sarà, di cui si legge
   ne' Maccabei; e come a quel fu molle
   suo re, così fia lui chi Francia regge."   (82–87)

("Soon after him shall come one from the West
   a lawless shepherd, one whose fouler deeds
   make him a fitting cover for us both.
He shall be another Jason, like the one
   in Maccabees: just as his king was pliant,
   so France's king shall soften to this priest.")

While we listen to Nicolas' words, we should remember that our Pilgrim is listening too, and Virgil is not only listening but watching his ward. And now the Pilgrim speaks:

Io non so s'io mi fui qui troppo folle,
 ch'i' pur rispuosi lui a questo metro:
  "Deh, or mi dì: quanto tesoro volle
Nostro Segnore in prima da san Pietro
 ch'ei ponesse le chiavi in sua balìa?
  Certo non chiese se non: 'Viemmi retro.'
Né Pier né li altri tolsero a Matia
 oro od argento, quando fu sortito
  al loco che perdé l'anima ria.
Però ti sta, ché tu se' ben punito;
 e guarda ben la mal tolta moneta
  ch'esser ti fece contra Carlo ardito!
E se non fosse ch'ancor lo mi vieta
 la reverenza de le somme chiavi
  che tu tenesti ne la vita lieta,
io userei parole ancor più gravi;
 ché la vostra avarizia il mondo attrista,
  calcando i buoni e sollevando i pravi.
Di voi pastor s'accorse il Vangelista,
 quando colei che siede sopra l'acque
  puttaneggiar coi regi a lui fu vista;
quella che con le sette teste nacque,
 e da le diece corna ebbe argomento
  fin che virtute al suo marito piacque.
Fatto v'avete dio d'oro e d'argento:
 e che altro è da voi a l'idolatre,
  se non ch'elli uno, e voi ne orate cento?
Ahi, Costantin, di quanto mal fu matre,
 non la tua conversion, ma quella dote
  che da te prese il primo ricco patre!" (88–117)

(I do not know, perhaps I was too bold here,
 but I answered him in tune with his own words:
  "Well tell me now: what was the sum of money

that holy Peter had to pay our Lord
  before He gave the keys into his keeping?
  Certainly He asked no more than 'Follow me.'
Nor did Peter or the rest extort gold coins
  or silver from Matthias when he was chosen
  to fill the place the evil one had lost.
So stay stuck there, for you are rightly punished
  and guard with care the money wrongly gained
  that made you stand courageous against Charles.
And were it not for the reverence I have
  for those highest of all keys that you once held
  in the happy life—if this did not restrain me,
I would use even harsher words than these,
  for your avarice brings grief upon the world,
  crushing the good, exalting the depraved.
You shepherds it was the Evangelist had in mind
  when the vision came to him of her who sits
  upon the waters playing whore with kings:
that one who with the seven heads was born
  and from her ten horns managed to draw strength
  so long as virtue was her bridegroom's joy.
You have built yourselves a God of gold and silver!
  How do you differ from the idolator,
  except he worships one, you worship hundreds?
Oh, Constantine, what evil did you sire,
  not by your conversion, but by the dower
  that the first wealthy Father got from you!'')

What an air of moral authority, what mastery of the situation, what majesty his words reveal![13] In line 97 he does not hesitate to say: "So stay stuck there, for you are rightly punished," putting his own seal on Divine Justice.[14]

    The second half of this canto reveals a picture of the Pilgrim completely different from that of the first half. Why has the poet offered these two utterly disparate pictures? Could it be because, knowing that in the second half of his canto he would present "himself" as such a lofty figure, his innate modesty and good taste and humor inspired him to construct, as a foil, a hesitant, tongue-tied, bewildered puppet moved by childish curiosity—or was there another motive? From the opening canto of the *Inferno* to the closing canto of the *Paradiso,* Dante presents his Pilgrim as continually learning, his development being one of the main themes of the poem; the progress is slow and there are even occasional backslidings. Perhaps the poet has wished to telescope or, rather, to prefigure, within the restricted limits of one canto, Canto XIX, the full gamut of his Pilgrim's potential spiritual development, the realization of which actually occupies the whole *Commedia.*

We must, then, see Dante the Pilgrim in this canto as one who has learned a lesson exceedingly well.[15] His teacher was Nicolas III, certainly one of the most distinguished sinners of the underworld. First of all he learns slowly, deductively, the answer to the question he first asked Virgil and was unable to ask Nicolas: "Chi è colui . . . ?" Secondly, from Nicolas' words and also from the spectacle he offers, the Pilgrim learns about the nature of a certain sin and the punishment which Divine Wisdom (*O somma sapienza . . .* !) has provided for the sin. Gazing with horror and revolted senses at the writhing, burning legs emerging from the holes, he has heard a simonist accuse himself and accuse his fellow simonists in terms that bespeak true *connaissance de cause.* But the Pilgrim was learning something else as he listened silently to Nicolas' lengthy, well-organized, and eloquent papal oration (we must smile as we remember that the Pilgrim had wondered if "it" could talk); he has learned the art of rhetoric. This is the first time in the *Inferno* that Dante the Pilgrim has "made a speech," and it is clearly patterned on Nicolas' style.

If, for example, Nicolas begins his discourse with the imperative "sappi," the Pilgrim also begins his with a command (introduced by the imperious "Deh") : "Deh, or mi dì" (90). If Nicolas uses the derivative verb *simmoneggiare* (74), the Pilgrim more than matches this with the resounding *puttaneggiare* (108). The Pope's closing words with their reference to the Bible are immediately fol-

lowed by the biblical reference which opens the Pilgrim's speech.[16]
Again, if Nicolas introduces the image of the purse "che su l'avere,
e qui me misi in borsa" (72), as receptacle on earth for his ill-
gotten gains and in Hell for his tortured body, the Pilgrim, who will
end his speech with the phrase "ricco patre" (117), speaks in
terms of *tesoro, moneta, oro,* and *argento*—as if contemptuously
flinging coins at the feet of Nicolas. And finally, if, in his first address to the Pilgrim, Nicolas indulges in a sarcastic rhetorical question (55–57): "Se' tu si tosto di quell' aver sazio?" the Pilgrim
begins by asking Nicolas, "quanto tesoro volle/Nostro Segnore in
prima da san Pietro/ch'ei ponesse le chiavi in sua balìa?"—both
questions concerned with money and wealth.

Of the three things the Pilgrim has learned from Nicolas, the
first is of course the least important; and, indeed, we can see how
the identity of Nicolas becomes less and less important for the
Pilgrim in the course of his speech—which falls into two equal
parts of fourteen lines each. In the first part (90–103) Nicolas is
personally addressed with the second person singular *tu* five times:
"or mi dì" (90); "Però ti sta, ché tu se' ben punito" (97); "e guarda
ben la mal tolta moneta" (98); and "che tu tenesti" (102). (Note
that in three of the five cases the Pilgrim addresses Nicolas with an
imperative.) In the last half of the speech, from 104–117, the second person plural *voi* is used, also five times: "la vostra avarizia"
(104); "Di voi pastor" (106); "Fatto v' avete Dio" (112); "e che
altro è da voi all' idolatre" (113); "e voi ne orate cento" (114).
The Pilgrim, then, in the second half of his speech, turns from the
individual Nicolas to address the full array of legs twisting in torment—whose presence, incidentally, we had forgotten. It was re-
marked earlier that at the beginning of our canto when the bolgia is
described—first the rocky topography, then the legs jutting out of
the rocks—it was the sinners *en masse* that were presented to us. It
was only from the Pilgrim's question to Virgil (the question that
never got answered directly) that we learned of the presence of one
individual who distinguished himself from the rest. From that mo-

ment on, nothing more was said of the other inhabitants: we are
made to focus on one pair of legs. But now, with the *voi* and *vostro,*
we are reminded again of the spectacle of the whole community of
simonists; it is not the individual sinner that counts, as the Pilgrim
has now learned, but the sin itself, represented by the anonymous
sinners. (It is precisely this that he failed to comprehend in Canto V
when he fainted from pity over the fate of an individual sinner.) It
is for this reason that the name of Nicolas is withheld throughout the
canto (the Pope being referred to as "colui che," "qual che," "qual
che se' che"). And it is only in the second part of his speech, addressed to "voi pastor," that Dante the Pilgrim analyzes the enormity of the sin of simony and its destructive consequences—to end
with an apostrophe to Constantine, in which the Emperor, supposedly the first to endow the Church with imperial rights, is sadly
rebuked for the part he unknowingly played in encouraging the sin
of simony. The almost tender lament, "Ahi, Constantine, di quanto
mal fu matre," parallels the wrathful, "O Simon Mago, o miseri
seguaci" of the first line of our canto, thereby bringing together, in
two apostrophes of historical import, the eponymous hero of the
simonists and his unwitting abettor, who made the Great Donation.
In this speech, and particularly in this apostrophe, the Pilgrim has
succeeded in echoing the tone of Dante the Poet.

No wonder Virgil is so pleased with his ward, as his smiling
face shows; no wonder that, the episode concluded, he begins the
ascent by embracing the Pilgrim with both arms:

> I' credo ben ch'al mio duca piacesse,
>   con sì contenta labbia sempre attese
>   lo suon de le parole vere espresse.
> Però con ambo le braccia mi prese,
>   e poi che tutto su mi s'ebbe al petto,
>   rimontò per la via onde discese.
> Né si stancò d'avermi a sé distretto,
>   sì men portò sovra 'l colmo de l'arco
>   che dal quarto al quinto argine è tragetto.

Quivi soavemente spuose il carco,
   soave per lo scoglio sconcio ed erto
   che sarebbe a le capre duro varco.
Indi un altro vallon mi fu scoperto. (121–133)

(I think my master liked what I was saying,
   for all the while he smiled and was intent
   on hearing the ring of truly-spoken words.
Then he took hold of me with both his arms,
   and when he had me firm against his breast,
   he climbed back up the path he had come down.
He did not tire of the weight clasped tight to him,
   but brought me to the top of the bridge's arch,
   the one that joins the fourth bank to the fifth.
And here he gently set his burden down—
   gently, for the ridge, so steep and rugged,
   would have been hard even for goats to cross.
From here another valley opened up.)

We had earlier noted the tender solicitude of Virgil in transporting his ward downward clasped to his hip; this time his appreciation of the Pilgrim's spiritual growth reveals itself with still greater tenderness: not only does he carry him all the way to the top showing no weariness, but takes care to set his precious burden down gently on the ridge.

Now that we are at the end of our canto, let us review two passages already briefly commented on. The first is the autobiographical incident in lines 16–21. All the commentators except Spitzer have assumed that this personal reminiscence was motivated by the poet's desire to exonerate himself: having committed an act that, on technical grounds, could be considered a sacrilege (destruction of church property), Dante would here be taking the opportunity to declare himself innocent of blame by pointing to the pure motivation of his act—evidently, because, so the commentators assume, this act, misinterpreted, had given rise to hostile rumors. And with line 21 "e questo sia suggel ch'ogn' omo sganni," Dante would be affixing the seal (*suggel*) onto his proclamation of innocence. We are asked, then, to believe that the simile introduced by Dante in his rescue-act, was a pretext for launching his statement of self-exoneration: it was only his desire to clear himself that made Dante create the topography of the third bolgia in imitation of a part of the Baptistry of San Giovanni!

First of all, there is not the slightest bit of evidence that any malicious rumors were circulated about the rescue-incident in which Dante took part (and it might be added that such an obviously humanitarian act would not be apt to give rise to such rumors). And even if they had been circulated, it would be most tasteless and inartistic for Dante to introduce a simile involving the Baptistry in Florence as an excuse for interpolating a plea of *not guilty*. As for the *suggel* of line 21, Spitzer sees in this no "seal" on a legal document; rather *suggel* should be interpreted in the general meaning of "type, stamp, pattern, image, or example"; it is only in this wider sense that the word is used throughout the *Commedia*. Spitzer also points out that the verb *sgannare* 'undeceive' in this line should be taken not in the narrow sense of 'correcting a specific misunderstanding,' but in the larger sense, with religious implications, of 'opening man's eyes to spiritual values.' Thus he would interpret line 21: "let this (*questo*), that is, let this picture which I am developing, be to you a revelation of the exemplary punishment (*suggel*) which may open the eyes of every man to the ultimate fate of sinners ('ch'ogn' omo saganni')."

In my opinion Spitzer is right as to the gratuitousness and tastelessness of the generally accepted interpretation of this passage. (In a recent English translation of the *Inferno* by Warwick Chipman, line 21 is given as "and so/I testify, that gossips doubt no more.") Nowhere else in the whole *Commedia* does Dante exploit the role of poet to plead in his own name for himself against his enemies. As to the artistic intent which Spitzer would attribute to the autobiographical interpolation, no one can doubt the realistic effect achieved by this personal reminiscence. I also accept his definition of *suggel* 'type, pattern, stamp, image, picture,' but I find it very difficult to agree with the indefinite reference he assumes for the pronoun *questo*. According to him, this pronoun would refer to the whole of the canto, pointing both backward to all that had been said in the preceding lines and forward to what is yet to be said—a function not easily imagined for a demonstrative pronoun. I prefer to limit the antecedent of *questo* to the two lines immediately preceding it. It must be, somehow, Dante's act in the Baptistry of San Giovanni that is intended as the image or picture that will open men's eyes to the truth—which could only mean, in this canto, the truth (or a truth) about simony. But how could this rescue-incident reveal a truth about simony?

First one must ask another question: why the *rupp' io* of line 20, whose explosive force destroys the tranquil beauty evoked by "nel mio bel San Giovanni?" In the single line devoted to the rescue-incident why need Dante mention and even stress the quite incidental detail of the necessary breaking of a receptacle in the Baptistry? What he did was the noble act of saving a human life, but with *rupp' io* coming at the beginning of the line the act of breaking seems to take precedence over the act of saving—and even over the plight of the victim ("un che dentro v'annegava"). Perhaps a later passage in this canto may shed light on this problem:

When Dante the Pilgrim, brought by Virgil to the bottom of the bolgia, addresses the twitching, upraised legs of Nicolas III, the sinner, mistaking him for Boniface, asks:

> . . . "Se' tu già costì ritto? . . .
> Se' tu sì tosto di quell'aver sazio
>   per lo qual non temesti tòrre a 'nganno
>   la bella donna, e poi di farne strazio?" (52–57)

In the bitter, rhetorical question which Nicolas intended for Boniface VIII there is an implicit description of simony offered by one simonist to another more infamous. According to this description, the simony of Boniface would consist of three offenses, the climactic one being that of "tearing" or "breaking": *e poi di farne strazio.*

It is surely no coincidence that twice in the canto the act of

breaking is placed in high relief. If Nicolas in line 57 presents
simony as the act of breaking, perhaps Dante already in line 21 was
preparing us to think in the same terms, and this line would mean:
let this (*questo*), that is, let the act of breaking be an image or picture (*suggel*) that will open men's eyes to the truth (*ogn' omo
sganni*), that is, to the true nature of simony.

If one wonders why the sin of fraud (for the Third Bolgia is one
of the subdivisions of the area where simple fraud is punished)
should here be overshadowed by that of "breaking" or destruction,
I would answer that the great sin is still fraud (and, indeed, Nicolas
specifically charges Boniface with fraud in line 56: *a inganno*)—
"breaking" is the result. Any individual who is fraudulent sins, but
when this sin appears in one who has taken Holy Orders, the result
of his fraud will be the destruction of Christ's Church—the greater,
the higher his office.

Granted the correctness of this interpretation, it is quite clear
why Dante took the pains to introduce and highlight the words
rupp' io. He was, in fact, taking the bold step of presenting his own
act as a technical parallel to the crimes of Boniface in order that the
simonist's sin of breaking, committed out of lust for treasure and
by means of deceit, would appear all the blacker by comparison with
Dante's destructive act performed out of love. The *inganno* of
line 56 is surely meant to recall the *sganni* of line 21; thus if, with
rupp' io, Dante would for a moment be suggesting a paradoxical
parallel between himself and the simonists, with the *sganni* of the
next line he would be offering the sharpest of contrasts to the
inganno of the simonists. And, for a moment (49), does not the
Pilgrim become a priest ("io stava come 'l frate che confessa . . ."),
since only a priest may commit simony?

The second passage to be examined for its relationship to the
canto as a whole is that contained in lines 7–30 describing the topography of the Third Bolgia and the bodies imprisoned in the
holes. The precision with which the proportions have been measured, in both cases, has already been mentioned. Surely this concern
with exact proportions is connected with the concept of "measure-

ment" as illustrated on another plane: the canto falls into two exact halves, reminding us in this respect of *Inferno* V, and the Pilgrim's devastatingly eloquent harangue of 28 lines falls into two parts of 14 lines each (the first containing five instances of *tu,* the second five instances of *voi*—as the speaker passes from the personal to the generic). Granted that this precision revealed on two different levels must indicate an intense concern with the idea of careful measurement, how can such an idea be significant for the canto as a whole?

It was said earlier that line 21: "e questo sia suggel che ogn' omo sganni" is inseparably connected with the meaning of the canto as a whole; and the definition of the word *suggel* proposed by Spitzer, and which I have accepted, was that of 'type, pattern, stamp, image, picture'—words that suggest the idea of an "exemplum," that is to say, the representation of a standard. And what is the act of "measuring" if not the application of a standard in assessing, in judging?

This is what the Pilgrim does in his judgment of Nicolas (anticipated in his description of his own act of breaking), which is the climax of Canto XIX; and the standard he applies is first that of the Son of God, then that of Peter, who conformed to the standard of Christ: Peter, the first predecessor of Nicolas, the Rock on which Christ built his Church which Nicolas strove to "break." So, in the first half of this carefully measured canto were introduced indications of measurement for the immediate purpose of precise description, but which point ahead to the symbolical measurement of Nicolas' sins by the Pilgrim.

After having attempted to show how the artistic structure of this canto serves to put into relief its moral teaching, let us now go outside our canto, for this teaching finds artistic support also in the form of parallels with other parts of the *Inferno:* one of the themes of XIX has been anticipated by a preceding incident, while its dominating image anticipates that of a later canto.

It was said earlier that the apostrophe with which our canto opens had no apparent connection with the narrative of the preceding canto, which had ended with Virgil pointing out to the Pilgrim the figure of Thäis, "scratching herself with shitty fingernails." But, though with the opening lines of Canto XIX there is a sudden break in the narrative, there is an unbroken subterranean continuity of theme. I say "subterranean continuity" for, apparently, the theme has suddenly shifted from the vice of flattery to that of simony; but the flatterer Thäis is, first of all, a whore ("la puttana"), and in the opening lines of our canto, in which the simonists are indicted, the one charge leveled against them is that of prostitution (*avolterate* as opposed to *di bontate . . . spose*). There is a suggestion of the sexual in lines 56–57, when Nicolas describes Boniface's sin as that of taking the Beautiful Lady by guile and tearing her asunder. And finally, "puttana" reappears in the form *puttaneggiar* of line 108, describing the Whore of Babylon, which to Dante represented the corrupt Church. It was pointed out earlier that the *simoneggiare* of Nicolas was capped by the *puttaneggiare* of the Pilgrim. But what is still more significant is the fact that the derivative verb *simoneggiare,* which must have been formed in imitation of *puttaneggiare* (there is no noun *simoneggio* in Italian), is the creation of Dante. Thus the poet would have allowed Nicolas to coin a word descriptive of his sin (*simoneggiare*), anticipating the *puttaneggiare* which will follow, but which must have already been in Dante's mind to serve as the basis for the coinage. And so the spirit of Thäis the whore, whose figure was so casually pointed out by Virgil at the end of Canto XVIII, pervades the atmosphere of Canto XIX.

The passage which our canto anticipates is found in the closing canto (XXXIV) of the *Inferno,* devoted so largely to the description of the monstrous body of Lucifer, held in an icy vise at the center of the earth. Virgil with the Pilgrim on his back proceeds slowly down the huge body to make his way out of Hell. As, descending "tuft by tuft," they reach the mid-point of Lucifer's hairy body, which marks (though of this the Pilgrim was not then aware) the center of the earth, Virgil, with great difficulty, reverses his position in the direction of Lucifer's legs ("volse la testa ov'elli avea le zanche" [79]), and at this point the descent turns into an ascent.[17]

After climbing a little farther along the haunch of Lucifer, Virgil with his burden reaches the crevice which affords a resting place. The Pilgrim, once seated there, raises his eyes—and, to his great bewilderment, sees the legs of Lucifer, raised upright, jutting from the crevice (85–90) :

> Poi uscì fuor per lo forò d'un sasso,
>> e puose me in su l'orlo a sedere;
>> appresso porse a me l'accorto passo.
> Io levai li occhi e credetti vedere
>> Lucifero com'io l'avea lasciato,
>> e vidili le gambe in sù tenere.

> (When he had got me through the rocky crevice,
>> he raised me to its edge and set me down,
>> then carefully he climbed and joined me there.
> I raised my eyes expecting I would see
>> the half of Lucifer I saw before,
>> instead I saw his two legs stretching upward.)

The legs of Lucifer rising upward from the crevice, like a magnified version of the upraised legs of Nicolas—this will be the last sight of Hell accorded the Pilgrim before he, with his guide, comes forth, to see again the stars.

If Dante saw fit to parallel the *contrappasso* of Nicolas, Christ's vicar who despoiled His Church, with that of the angel who rebelled against God Himself (if, after measuring him with the standard of Christ, he would be comparing the enormity of his guilt to that of Lucifer), little wonder that Canto XIX is inspired by such intensity of moral wrath and that such elaborate devices of narrative technique were employed to enhance this intensity.

⚜ ⚜

Canto XIX, from beginning to end, is totally devoted to a condemnation of the sin being punished in the Third Bolgia. In none of the many cantos dealing with the varieties of Fraud are we made to

feel such concentration on a moral message. As for the cantos dealing with Incontinence, the reader will think immediately of the
first half of Canto V which contains nothing but the pitiless description (beginning with "Stavvi Minòs orribilmente, e ringhia") of
the punishment inflicted on the sinners and the condemnatory words
of Virgil. And though in the second half there is created an atmosphere of tender intimacy, and we hear only the dulcet tones of Francesca's revelations, the reader is meant to sense that the stern
teaching of the first half continues as the foundation upon which the
canto as a whole is built. Surely, Canto V, like XIX, is devoted from
beginning to end to a condemnation of the sin in question: in the
second half the shrewd moralist poet has simply shifted his tactics:
after having represented Lust in all its potential horror, he shows
the sweetly insidious danger of this vice through the words of Francesca who had succumbed to it, which lure the Pilgrim into imitating
her weakness.

If I am right in believing that Cantos V and XIX are the only
two in the *Divine Comedy* devoted exclusively to an analytical exposure of sin, we must wonder about the choice that Dante made.
Perhaps Lust, the least heinous of sins, was chosen because it is the
one to which Everyman is apt to be the most susceptible. It is, or may
be, the most private of sins. To the sin of simony only men of a
special caste are susceptible, but its consequences are a public scandal
involving the destruction of God's Church.

Dante and Virgil behind the Heavenly messenger, who opens the gates of Dis; the three Furies on the battlements. Canto IX, *Inferno*. From the Vatican, Biblioteca Apostolica, MS Latino 4776. Florentine, ca. 1390-1400.

IV

At the Gates of Dis

WHEN Beatrice came, Christ came. Most critics recognize the final Advent of Christ in the Coming of Beatrice to judge her lover in *Purgatory* XXX. I believe that the First Advent of Christ and the Second are also present in the *Divine Comedy:* in *Inferno* IX and *Purgatory* VIII, respectively.[1]

Now it may be said that each of these two cantos appears in the same place in its canticle—that is, if we consider Canto I of the *Inferno* as an introduction to the whole poem (which would leave 33 cantos in the *Inferno* proper to correspond with the 33 of the *Purgatory* and of the *Paradise*). And not only do *Inferno* IX and *Purgatory* VIII appear in the "same place," but the events treated in each lead to similar developments in the Pilgrim's journey: the action in *Inferno* IX precedes his entrance into the City of Dis; that in *Purgatory* VIII precedes his entrance into the gate of Purgatory proper.

Moreover, in both cantos the poet interrupts the narrative with a tercet inviting the reader to penetrate to the doctrine hidden behind the veil of his words:

> O voi ch'avete li 'ntelletti sani,
> mirate la dottrina che s'asconde
> sotto 'l velame de li versi strani. (*Inferno* IX, 61–63)

> (O all of you whose intellects are sound,
> look now and see the meaning that is hidden
> beneath the veil that covers my strange verses)

Aguzza qui, lettor, ben li occhi al vero,
  ché 'l velo è ora ben tanto sottile,
  certo che 'l trapassar dentro è leggero. (*Purgatory* VIII, 19–21)

(Here, reader, sharpen well your eyes to the truth
  for, now, the veil is so transparent
  that, certainly, seeing through it is an easy matter).

Of the many "addresses to the reader" in the *Divine Comedy* these
are the only ones in which we are explicitly asked to interpret the
literal sense of the narrative figuratively; accordingly, we should see
the two passages in sharper parallel than is usually done. In fact,
that Dante in the second passage was remembering his earlier admonition to the reader and was expecting his reader to remember it
too, is suggested by the *ora* of line 20: "Reader, the veil *now* is
surely so transparent that it is easy to penetrate." That is, the reader
"now" is being offered an easier mystery to solve than he was in the
passage of *Inferno* IX (where the word *velame* appears instead of
the "più sottile *velo*" of the second passage.)[2]

What is the mystery that Dante each time is asking the reader
to solve? The first passage is immediately followed by the appearance
of an angel who opens the gate of the City of Dis; the second, by the
appearance of two angels in the Valley of the Princes, sent to put
the serpent to flight. That the parallel between the two angelic events
has been overlooked is easily explained: whereas Dante's admonition to the reader in *Purgatory* VIII had been taken by the critics to
refer to what follows (since what preceded was nothing remarkable), that of *Inferno* IX has mainly been taken to refer to what
preceded—the sudden, startling appearance of the three Furies on
the top of the tower, screaming and calling upon Medusa to come
and turn the Pilgrim to stone.[3] But since the admonitory tercet of
Purgatory VIII must refer to what follows, it is only natural to assume, given the parallelisms already pointed out, that the same holds
true for *Inferno* IX.[4] And I believe that Dante, in asking us to consider the deep significance of the two angelic interventions, is asking
us to think of the First and Second Advents of Christ.

Of the two parallels involved, that between the event in *Purgatory* VIII and the Second Advent can be more easily demonstrated: unlike the angelic intervention before the gates of Dis, the appearance of the angels in the Valley is presented as an habitual occurrence. Every day, at the same time of day, the angels come to wait for the serpent, who always comes and is always driven away. There could hardly be a clearer symbolization of Christ's daily coming into the hearts of those ready to receive him.

The coming of the angel in *Inferno* IX to save the Pilgrim (who is Everyman) was a unique event, as was the First Advent, the Coming of Christ to save mankind. But there is more than this simple detail to suggest that Dante is thinking here in terms of the First Advent: at the end of Canto VIII Virgil reminds his ward of the devils' failure to prevent Christ's entrance into Hell—referring, that is, to the Harrowing of Hell. This event was the culmination of Christ's life on earth, completing the miracle of His Coming, of His First Advent. In fact, St. Bernard defines the First Coming in terms of the descent into Hell; it is as if he sees in this Advent "one act of coming" uniting Heaven, Earth and Hell.[5]

Taking for granted, then, that *Inferno* IX contains an enactment of the First Advent, and *Purgatory* VIII of the Second, let us study carefully in each case what precedes them in the text, in order to see the way in which the poet leads up to the moment of angelic intervention. Given the portentous significance of these two events (the only ones in the *Divine Comedy* whose veiled significance Dante has explicitly asked his reader beforehand to ponder), it is surely to be expected that the poet has striven with particular care to prepare for them in such a way as to set them into relief.

In order to follow the path leading to the First Advent let us begin by reviewing the events of Canto VIII. When this canto opens, the Pilgrim and his guide have come to the shore of the river Styx on the other side of which lies the City of Dis; Virgil has pointed out to him the figures of the Wrathful in the muddy waters, announcing the presence, beneath the water, of the Slothful, who are sending up bubbles through the mud. Suddenly the Pilgrim's eyes are attracted

to the top of a tower by two flames issuing forth, and he sees another
light from very far away flash back as if in response. To the Pilgrim's bewildered question Virgil answers enigmatically that he
should already be able to see "quello che s' aspetta." The Pilgrim
looks over the waters to see Phlegyas swiftly approaching, shouting,
"Now I've got you!"[6] Virgil rebukes him disdainfully; the two
travellers enter the boat and soon arrive at the other shore, their
passage being interrupted by the encounter with Filippo Argenti.[7]
"Usciteci" cries Phlegyas landing the boat at a certain point, "qui è
l'entrata." They disembark and the Pilgrim sees thousands of devils
massed upon the walls of Dis.

The demons greet his appearance with angry yells. Then begins
a period of uncertainty for the Pilgrim and uncertainty for Virgil.
In answer to the screams Virgil signals his wish to speak to the angry
host secretly (a second time we are told of a signal given, and a
second time there is a suggestion of secrecy). The Pilgrim's fear
begins when he hears the condition imposed by the devils: that
while Virgil may come to the gates for the parley, the Pilgrim must
return alone from where he had come—that is, back to the "dark
wood" of Canto I. Virgil, as we expect, is very calm and patiently
reassuring; but when, after his brief talk with the devils (which the
Pilgrim and the reader do not hear), the gates of Dis are slammed
shut in his face, then, for the first time—in fact, for the only time
in the *Divine Comedy*—Virgil gives signs not only of bewilderment
but of discouragement about his mission. And the Pilgrim hears
him sigh:

> Li occhi a la terra, e le ciglia avea rase
>   d'ogne baldanza, e dicea ne' sospiri:
>   "Chi m'ha negate le dolenti case!"   (118–120)
>
> (With eyes downcast, all self-assurance now
>   erased from his brow, sighing, he said: "Who are these
>   to forbid my entrance to the halls of grief!")

Nevertheless, he insists that victory will be theirs; the devils will be
defeated as they were once before when Christ came to open the

gates of Hell; in fact, as he tells his frightened ward, someone is now on the way to them, "tal che per lui ne fia la terra aperta." After this prophecy which closes Canto VIII, he becomes silent, seeming to listen—for what sound we do not know. And as he waits he starts muttering to himself, rather incoherently:

> "Pur a noi converrà vincer la punga,"
>   cominciò el, "se non . . . Tal ne s'offerse!
>   Oh quanto tarda a me ch'altri qui giunga!" (IX, 7–9)

> ("But surely we were meant to win this fight,"
>   he began, "or else . . . But, such help was promised!
>   O how much time it's taking him to come!")

It seems strange that after having predicted the arrival of their savior his first words should indicate the possibility of defeat (. . . *se non* . . . !); he has to remind himself of the power of the one who "offered herself" (*Tal ne s'offerse*). He ends with a note of impatient yearning for the arrival he had just predicted. Such indications of indecision on the part of his leader have a calamitous effect on the Pilgrim; but, hoping for the best, he asks a discreetly probing question of his guide: had anyone from Limbo ever before penetrated the abyss of Lower Hell? Virgil, well aware of the motive that prompted the Pilgrim's question, answers that he himself, soon after his death, had descended to the very bottom of Hell, bidden by Erichtho to fetch a soul up from the depths. He ends his account with words of encouragement: "ben so il cammin: però ti fa sicuro." While he is describing the terrain where they find themselves— quite casually, as if to kill time as they wait—the Pilgrim's attention is suddenly diverted by a horrid spectacle: on the top of the tower there spring up before his eyes the figures of the three Furies, whose terrible, bloody aspect horrifies and unnerves him. Virgil's overt reaction to the apparition hardly allows us access to his feelings: he merely identifies the figures for the Pilgrim's benefit and then becomes silent. They watch the Furies tear their breasts, beating themselves; they hear their screams, calling for Medusa to make her appearance—and, at this point, Virgil completely loses his composure, saying:

> "Volgiti 'n dietro e tien lo viso chiuso;
>   ché se 'l Gorgón si mostra e tu 'l vedessi,
>   nulla sarebbe di tornar mai suso." (55–57)

> ("Now turn your back and cover up your eyes,
>   for if the Gorgon comes and you should see her,
>   there would be no returning to the world!")

As a further indication of his panic, and as if doubting the efficacy of his own words to the Pilgrim, Virgil turns him around and places his own hands on top of the Pilgrim's, which were already covering his closed eyes (58–60). Surely every hope of the angel's arrival (or at least of the successful outcome of his arrival) has vanished from Virgil's mind: if Medusa could be summoned by the Furies to cross the Pilgrim's path, if her magic could function as it had in Pagan times before Christ came, there could be no functioning of Christian machinery.

But immediately after Virgil's total submission to Pagan laws (line 60), the sounds announcing the angel's approach are heard. One tercet, however, separates what might have been the triumph of Paganism from the actual triumph of Christianity: the address to the reader calling upon him for the true interpretation of *li strani versi* yet to come (61–63). It could be said that this tercet is the dividing line between B.C. time and A.D. time. Now Virgil can remove his hands from the Pilgrim's eyes, enabling him to see the figure of the heavenly messenger passing over the Styx. He sees him open the gates with a light touch of his wand, he hears his scornful word to the devils, and watches his departure. The travellers enter through the gates opened for them: the Pilgrim, full of curiosity, looks around him, and the canto ends with the kind of question that has become familiar to the reader—"Maestro, quai son quelle genti . . .?" It is, somehow, as if nothing has happened, as if the Pilgrim's journey to Beatrice and to God had not seemed for a few terrible moments to have been placed in jeopardy.

It was, of course, Virgil's defeatist attitude that was responsible for the interval of despair. How is his attitude to be explained? His despondency after the devils have shut the gates of Dis in his face is accepted by most scholars as quite understandable: for the first time he has met with resistance that he is unable to cope with. But there are two objections against this explanation. First, why was Virgil unable to cope with the resistance of the devils? It would seem that even before his failure to quell their turbulence, his attitude was such as to seem to anticipate failure. Why should Virgil wish to speak privately with the devils, and express this desire by means of sign-language? When he heard the devils screaming "Chi è costui . . .?" why did he not answer them sternly with the words that had proved effective earlier with Charon and Minos: "Vuolsi così colà dove si puote,/ciò che si vuole, e più non dimandare," instead of gesturing mutely? In fact, this formula with its concluding words "e più non dimandare," is even more appropriate here than it was on the previous occasions, for only here does the enemy ask a question. (Charon and Minos had uttered hostile warnings; it is interesting that here the devils who will get the better of Virgil, temporarily, do not begin by uttering threats with signs of overt hostility.) It is as if the formula which, by way of anticipation, had proved successful was actually conceived for this occasion, and Virgil failed at this crucial point to use it.[8]

Secondly, even if we accept as natural Virgil's immediate reaction of dejection when the gates are slammed in his face, we must remember that very soon afterwards, at the end of Canto VIII, he predicts to the Pilgrim their rescue through divine intervention; why, then, do fresh doubts assail him in the following canto? He struggles against them (. . . *Tal ne s'offerse!*), but why does he have to struggle (his prophecy of the coming of the "Veltro" at the end of Canto I was attended by no such doubts)? He will show confidence once again when he speaks of his earlier, successful descent into Hell; but when the Furies suddenly appear on top of the tower to call Medusa, his collapse is total. We have seen that for one crucial moment, before Dante the Poet interrupts the narrative to address his reader, Virgil does actually believe in the supremacy of Pagan forces.

There can be no doubt that up until the address to the reader the atmosphere of Cantos VIII and IX has become more and more the atmosphere of Pagan mythology, with which Virgil in his lifetime was so familiar. Surely the City of Dis must have reminded him of his own Tartarus, because of their parallel functions in the Christian and Pagan otherworldly penal systems, respectively. Moreover, when he saw the iron wall of Dis, he may have remembered the iron tower and doorposts of the Tartarus he himself had described in the *Aeneid;* and he knew that the gates of the Pagan Lower Hell could never be forced. Thus, when the gates of Dis were slammed in his face, this might well have seemed to have an ominous significance. It is true that by the time he reaches the Pilgrim's side he is able to predict the coming of the angel, but if, immediately after (7–9), he is able to doubt again, perhaps he remembered that he himself had written of the gates of Tartarus that not even one sent from Heaven could open them:

> Porta adversa ingens solidoque adamante columnae,
> vis et nulla virum, non ipsi exscindere bello
> coelicolae valeant... (*Aeneid* VI, 552–4.)

> (In front, a huge gate and columns of solid adamant
> which no human force, not the gods themselves,
> are strong enough to pull down in war ...)

He had also described the bloodstained figure of Tesiphone seated on the iron tower forever on guard, and suddenly he sees spring up, on the top of the tower of Dis, the bloody Tesiphone flanked by her bloody sisters; and he hears them call for Medusa.

Here, with the screams of the three Furies directed to an unseen creature offstage, it is as if the world of mythology has come to life again, and the machinery of Paganism is once again set in motion. The three Furies are obviously not the only creatures of mythology who inhabit Dante's Inferno, but all the rest of them, scattered from the beginning to the end of Hell, are simply remnants of antiquity allowed to survive in order to play some part (if only a representational role, e.g. the Minotaur) in the workings of Divine Justice; they are exiled from their own world to live in the Christian world of Dante's Hell, in the atmosphere of the Hell Dante created. But the Furies bring their own atmosphere, and they work in opposition to the Divine Plan. Moreover, when they decide to call upon Medusa to play her customary role, they almost make us believe (there is no doubt that they did make Virgil believe) that any mythological monster might suddenly appear on stage. And, with their reminiscence (54) of Theseus: ("Mal non vengiammo in Teseo l'assalto!")⁹ it is as if the Pilgrim himself is sucked into the vortex of alien forces: the Pilgrim is to be the Furies' next victim after Theseus! And it is from this Pagan fate that Virgil, desperate, hysterical, seeks to save his ward! But this Pagan drama so suddenly set in motion is just as suddenly swept off-stage by the earthquake announcing the coming of the angel.

Now the coming of the angel in which Virgil could not quite believe is a re-enactment of the First Coming of Christ. And here we have the main reason why Virgil could not quite believe, and was so susceptible to reminders of the world he had written about in his lifetime. We must remember that Virgil is in the Inferno, not only for a short space of time, as the guide of Dante's Pilgrim, but also, and for eternity, as one of the damned—his "sin" being that of not believing in the coming of the Messiah. Like all those in Limbo at the time, he had witnessed the Harrowing of Hell; like them he learned that Christ has come. And it was surely his remembering of that event in Canto VIII that made possible the revelation to him of the angel's approach, for his announcement of the advent immediately follows his reminder to the Pilgrim of Christ's triumph. But because during his lifetime he could not believe in the coming of Christ, so now he can not quite believe in the coming of the angel —in spite of his having learned from Beatrice that the Pilgrim's journey is willed in Heaven.

In fact if we accept, as any interpreter of Dante's poem must accept it, the medieval belief that Virgil in the *Fourth Eclogue* had prophesied the birth of Christ, then we can find in the historical Virgil thus reinterpreted, something of a parallel to his "belief–nonbelief" attitude illustrated in our canto: for when he wrote the prophecy he himself did not know what he was prophesying.[10] In some mysterious way he had been used by the God he never knew to proclaim a truth he could not have believed in.[11]

Thus, in our canto, Virgil is made to repeat, to "imitate" the defect that doomed him to Limbo. From my analysis it would seem clear that ever since he caught sight of the gates of Dis he has been acting out of character. The reader has become so accustomed to Virgil's role as infallible guide and mentor that it comes as a shock to see the figure that he cuts in Cantos VIII and IX. It is as if he has a new role in the drama—or a role in some other drama. It is only after the sounds of the earthquake heralding the angel's approach have died away and Virgil removes his hands from the Pilgrim's eyes, telling him exactly where to direct his glance, that we recognize again the Virgil we have come to know.

Why was Virgil made to undergo such a humiliating experience? From the moral point of view the purpose may well have been to demonstrate the weakness of Reason when not accompanied by Faith. But it is also true that Virgil's behavior is made to serve artistic purposes; it is obvious, for example, that his inner disequilibrium, with its possible threatening consequences, adds suspense and excitement to the narration—as well as an ironical undertone: with Phlegyas, Virgil had been completely the master of the situation, and with Filippo Argenti, peremptory and contemptuous; with the Pilgrim whom he embraces approvingly he had spoken words of eloquent solemnity blessing the womb that bore him. Thus, the sharpest of contrasts is offered by the inglorious role he will play in the scene that follows. But the treatment of Virgil also serves a more deeply significant auctorial goal: Virgil had to fail in order that the *messo* could be sent. For Dante the Poet wishes to have the First Advent represented somewhere in the *Inferno*. And Virgil had to fail when he did, after landing from Phlegyas' boat in front of the City of Dis, so that "gates" could be brought into play: gates open, then shut fast, then open again.[12]

Now since Virgil failed, the angel had to come for the sake of the Pilgrim. But to think only in these terms would give too narrow a perspective, for the success of the Pilgrim's journey was guaranteed from the beginning. Nothing actually could have prevented him from reaching his goal, so that if, on the one hand, the coming of the *messo* was necessary for his sake, it was made necessary quite artificially—in order that the First Advent could be represented. As was just said, Virgil had to fail so that the angel could come. And so, the answer to Virgil's bewildered question "Chi m'ha negate le dolenti case?" is—Dante the Poet.

The uneventful entrance of the two travelers into the City of Dis, once the *messo* had opened the gates with his wand, is announced in Canto IX, 106: "Dentro li entrammo sanz'alcuna guerra." Actually, this announcement could have come much earlier: if Dante the Poet had not wanted to introduce a re-enactment of the First Advent, they would have passed through the gates in Canto VIII a few lines after the devil's jeering question in lines 84–85:

> . . . "Chi è costui che sanza morte
> va per lo regno de la morta gente?"
>
> (. . . "Who is the one approaching? Who, without death,
> dares walk into the kingdom of the dead?")

The following tercet (86-88) could well have been devoted to Virgil's stern rebuke and his repetition of the awesome formula that could never fail: "Vuolsi così colà. . . ." And perhaps in the next line (89) we would have read "Dentro li entrammo sanz'alcuna guerra." This is what would have been required by the laws that had operated up to Canto VIII, 86, of the *Inferno,* but because Dante decided as he did, those "laws" had to be superseded temporarily by other laws: we are for a moment no longer in the confines of the story of the *Divine Comedy* but in the wider reaches of sacred history, somehow caught up in the battle between the forces of

Paganism and those of Christianity. But because of drama of Paganism, re-awakened to be vanquished by Christianity, has to take place on a stage set up within the confines of the story, the effect is somewhat that of a puppet-show—which begins like a dumb show: we remember Virgil's mute gesture that starts the action, and the conclave of voices we ate not allowed to hear. Virgil is a puppet whose strings are pulled to make him go now forward, now backward, or simply to twitch (mentally). The three raging Furies who pop up suddenly on the top of the tall tower are puppets pretending to call upon another puppet offstage (Medusa).

And surely the arrival of the *messo* is pure theater: as Virgil in frantic desperation covers the eyes of his ward (and Dante the Poet intervenes to bid his reader interpret carefully) a thunderous sound is heard causing the land to tremble; three tercets are devoted to a description of the fearful repercussions. This tumult of sounds is followed by tumultuous movement as the thousands of panic-stricken souls in the marsh dive to the bottom of the muddy water, hiding from the heavenly being whom the Pilgrim now sees approaching with minimal, mechanically rhythmical movements:

> Come le rane innanzi a la nimica
>   biscia per l'acqua si dileguan tutte,
>   fin ch'a la terra ciascuna s'abbica,
> vid' io più di mille anime distrutte
>   fuggir così dinanzi ad un ch'al passo
>   passava Stige con le piante asciutte.
> Dal volto rimovea quell' aere grasso,
>   menando la sinistra innanzi spesso;
>   e sol di quell' angoscia parea lasso. (76–84)

> (As frogs before their enemy, the snake,
>   all scatter through the pond and then dive down
>   until each one is squatting on the bottom,
> so I saw more than a thousand fear-shocked souls
>   in flight, clearing the path of one who came
>   walking the Styx, his feet dry on the water.

    From time to time with his left hand he fanned
      his face to push the putrid air away,
      and this was all that seemed to weary him.)

The *messo* comes as energy and power and, finally, eloquence; hence, the reader hears the sound of his coming and sees the effects of his coming before he is made aware of "un, ch'al passo/passava Stige con le piante asciutte." And when he has arrived his appearance is not described. It is with a mere tap of his wand, a token gesture, that he opens the gates (note the diminutive *verghetta* used of the wand) and, after his scathing rebuke to the devils (he makes the kind of speech that Virgil should have and could have made), he goes back whence he had come. Of course he does not address the Pilgrim and his guide whom he has saved, nor does he in any way acknowledge their presence—as little as any actor before moving off-stage would address a member of his audience. Now that the show is over the two travellers can enter the gates to continue the journey that was willed by God—as Virgil for one brief moment, with his hands over the Pilgrim's eyes, seemed to have completely forgotten.

    If the narrative leading up to the advent of the *messo* is unique in the treatment of Virgil and in what this treatment entailed, it is also unique because of the artistic technique involving the matter of narrative time. According to my summary, these events began with the opening lines of Canto VIII; it would also be possible to go back still farther to include the final lines of Canto VII. Virgil's interpretation of the gurgling words sung by the Slothful beneath the mud, end with the lines 125–126: ". . . Quest' inno si gorgoglian ne la strozza, / che dir nol posson con parola integra." They are immediately followed by four lines of narrative that close the canto:

      Così girammo de la lorda pozza
        grand'arco, tra la ripa secca e 'l mézzo,
        con li occhi vòlti a chi del fango ingozza.
      Venimmo al piè d'una torre al da sezzo. (VII, 127–130)

(Then making a wide arc we walked around
   the pond between the dry bank and the slime,
   our eyes still fixed on those who gobbled mud.
We came, in time, to the foot of a high tower.)

Line 130 has no exact parallel in the *Inferno* as a final line of a canto. It is true that there are five other cantos which end, as this does, with the announcement of the point reached.[13]

E vengo in parte ove non è che luca. (IV, 151)

(I come into a place where no light is.)

Venimmo al punto dove si digrada:
quivi trovammo Pluto, il gran nemico. (VI, 114–115)

(and came to where the ledge begins descending;
there we found Plutus, mankind's arch-enemy.)

  . . . e gimmo inver lo mezzo
per un sentier ch'a una valle fiede,
che 'nfin là sù facea spiacer suo lezzo. (X, 134–136)

  (. . . we headed toward the center by a path
that strikes into a vale, whose stench arose
disgusting us as high up as we were.)

Noi passamm' oltre . . .
. . . infino in su l'altr' arco
che cuopre 'l fosso in che si paga il fio
a quei che scommettendo acquistan carco. (XXVII, 133–136)

(My guide and I moved farther on . . .
. . . until we stood on the next arch
that spans the fosse where penalties are paid
by those who, sowing discord, earned Hell's wages.)

E quindi uscimmo a riveder le stelle. (XXXIV, 139)

(and we came out to see once more the stars.)

But there is an important difference between these five endings and that of Canto VII: none of these leave the reader in suspense. In none of them are we suddenly offered the outlines of a landscape-marker for which we were unprepared. This high tower seems to come from nowhere, just as the high mountain in the opening canto of the *Inferno* (I,13) came from nowhere (*Ma poi ch'i' fui al piè d'un colle giunto*).

And the lines that follow in the narrative, that is, the opening lines of Canto VIII, also have no parallel:

> Io dico, seguitando, ch'assai prima
> che noi fossimo al piè de l'alta torre,
> li occhi nostri n'andar suso a la cima
> per due fiammette che i vedemmo porre ... (VIII, 1–4)

> (I must explain, however, that before
> we finally reached the foot of that high tower,
> our eyes had been attracted to its summit
> by two small flames we saw flare up just there ...)

For the first and only time in the *Inferno,* Dante interrupts the line of his narrative, turning back in time in order to tell his reader what had taken place before the point reached in the preceding statement—that is, between Virgil's words about the sinners in the mud (VII, 115–24) and his arrival with his ward at the foot of the tower (VII, 130). Just what did take place in that interval of time? It is not too clear just when, in Canto VIII, we have caught up with the narrative time of the last line of Canto VII. Let us briefly resume the events of Canto VIII:

> The signal-lights are seen (1–12) ; then Phlegyas appears screaming (13–18). He is rebuked by Virgil (19–24), and the two travellers start off in his boat across the Styx (25–30) ; after the episode with Filippo Argenti (31–66) the Pilgrim and his guide approach the City of Dis (67–78) and are left in front of the gates (79–81). Virgil fails to gain entrance into the City (82–130).

The first guess that the reader is apt to make is that only the brief episode of the signal-lights is included in the interval of time posited: discussing the lights they have just seen, the travellers reach the tower as Phlegyas is approaching. We must assume with this interpretation that the tower is on the hither side of the Stygian marsh, and that they would leave the tower behind as they cross the Styx.[14]

Now Steiner, for one, believes that the tower mentioned in Canto VII, 130, was not on this side; he states in his commentary to this line that it is one of the towers of the City of Dis seen across the Styx. But this is an impossible interpretation: *if the river Styx were between the two travellers and the tower* we would not have been told that they had gotten to the foot of it. And from the way the story is told the reader is led to believe that the tower is on the shore from which the two travellers had first caught sight of the Wrathful; in the last four lines of Canto VII we are told that they walked a while following the curve of the shore and, then, that they came to the foot of a high tower. Accordingly, the shift in the time of the narrative would have been introduced in order to inform us that, just before reaching this tower, the Pilgrim had seen a signal light at its top (answered by another some distance away), and to tell us of the brief dialogue between the Pilgrim and his guide. Thus, with line 12 we would have caught up with the final line of Canto VII—for in line 13 Phlegyas begins to appear who will take them across the Styx.

But there are several objections against this interpretation. Why are we not told more about this tower that the Pilgrim and his guide came upon so suddenly? Not only does it appear out of nowhere, it seems to disappear immediately into nothingness: after the last line of Canto VII there is no further reference to it—that is, no additional information about a tower on this side of the Styx. Moreover, the problematic interval of time that the reader must fill out cannot be accounted for in terms of the brief event noted in lines 1–12 of Canto VIII, because of the words ". . . *assai* prima / che noi fossimo al piè de l'alta torre": it was not just before the arrival at the foot of the tower that the signal-lights were seen, but a considerable time before (note also the last three words of Canto VII, *al da sezzo,* 'finally'). And, indeed, Dante would hardly have exploited this exceptional device of "backward then forward movement in time" merely to put into relief the detail of the signal-lights.

We must, then, revise our picture of what happened before the arrival at the mysterious tower, by including a longer series of events in the interval posited. These events would comprehend not only the incident of the signal-lights but also the arrival of Phlegyas, the words exchanged between him and Virgil, their entrance into the boat, their voyage across the Styx interrupted by the incident of Filippo Argenti, and the final words of Phlegyas in line 81: "Usciteci! . . . qui è l'intrata!" It would be line 81, then, that would bring us up to date with the last line of Canto VII—which does indeed refer to one of the towers of Dis, but not seen across the Styx, for in the last line of Canto VII Virgil and the Pilgrim have already crossed it and are on the other side. Of course, in the first lines of Canto VIII which go back in time, they have not yet come to the tower, they have not yet crossed the river; and it is, indeed, from across the Styx that the tall tower with its signal lights was first seen—long before they arrived there!

Thus, Dante has deliberately confused the reader, has deliberately, and surely for artistic purposes, blurred the focus of the sequence of events and has dislocated time. When the tower is first mentioned the reader will naturally believe that the two travellers come upon it in the course of their walk along the Stygian shore, and we instinctively read into the last lines of Canto VII the meaning: "we walked . . . until we came . . . ," not noticing that the announcement of arrival has been worded "we walked . . . we came after a long time." And up to line 13 of Canto VIII the reader will believe that only the sight of the signal-fires has preceded what is predicated in the closing line of Canto VII and that, with the arrival of Phlegyas, events will move ahead from that point on. It is only when we begin wondering why more has not been made of the tower that was supposedly left behind on the other shore that we

will be slowly forced into the correct reconstitution of events, and
will see that in the last line of Canto VII the Pilgrim has already
crossed the river Styx with Phlegyas, and has heard his command to
get out; it is only in line 82 of Canto VIII that the narrative will
start moving ahead in time, as the Pilgrim looks up and sees the
thousands of devils amassed upon the walls of Dis:

> ("Usciteci," gridò, "qui è l'intrata.")
> Io vidi più di mille in su le porte
>   da ciel piovuti, che stizzosamente
>   dicean: "Chi è costui che sanza morte . . . ?"   (VIII, 81–84)

> (. . . "Get out! Here is the entrance."
> I saw more than a thousand fiendish angels
>   perching above the gates enraged, screaming
>   "Who is the one approaching? Who, without death . . . ?")

Note how swiftly the sight of the devils follows upon the cry of
Phlegyas in 81—uttered before the Pilgrim and Virgil have dis-
embarked. Their subsequent landing on the shore is not predicated.
We have already been told (Canto VII, 130) that they came to the
foot of a high tower. And it must be from the foot of this tower
(though the poet withholds this information from us at this point)
that the Pilgrim, looking up, sees the devils swarming over the top
of the gates. He is still there in Canto IX, when he sees the Furies
on the tower's summit:

> E altro disse, ma non l'ho a mente;
>   però che l'occhio m'avea tutto tratto
>   ver' l'alta torre a la cima rovente,
> dove in un punto furon dritte ratto
>   tre furïe infernal di sangue tinte . . .   (IX, 34–38)

> (And he said other things, but I forget them;
>   for suddenly my eyes were drawn above,
>   up to the fiery top of that high tower
> where in no time at all and all at once
>   sprang up three hellish Furies stained with blood . . .)

That this "high tower" is the same as the one mentioned in Canto VII, 130, there can be no doubt, if only because of the presence of the definite article. This is not *a* high tower, but *the* high tower last mentioned in Canto VIII, 2 (". . . prima / che noi fossimo al piè de l'alta torre").[15]

So, in the last line of Canto VII, the author, projecting his story ahead, brings his characters to the foot of a high tower which, actually, in the course of the step-by-step narrative, they do not reach until 81 lines later.[16] And the reader himself does not know that they have made good the last line of Canto VII until he comes to the reference to "the tower" in line 36 of Canto IX—after a number of events have taken place in the shadow of the tower.[17]

After the reader has reconstructed the events that must have preceded the arrival at the tower (and *only* then), and has come to realize that the tower is on the "other" side of the Styx, he can, on turning back to reread the last line of Canto VII, receive the full impact of the suddenness of the arrival announced there—an impact completely imperceptible the first time he reads the narrative lines beginning with the casual assurance of *così,* that close the canto:

> Così girammo de la lorda pozza
> grand'arco, tra la ripa secca e 'l mézzo,
> con li occhi vòlti a chi del fango ingozza.
> Venimmo al piè d'una torre al da sezzo. (VII, 127–130)

Granted that this impact could be achieved only by the postponement of the reader's reconstruction of events, why should Dante want to achieve this effect? Surely, it was in order to strike the note of inevitability.[18]

In describing the events leading up to the re-enactment of the First Advent, Dante the poet has introduced two innovations neither of which he is going to repeat in the course of the *Comedy* and which, at first glance, might seem to have nothing in common. One involves character delineation—the strange behavior of Virgil; the other is the use of a device of narrative technique: a forward-back-

ward-forward movement in time. Actually, of course the two innovations are closely related. Both represent temporary dislocations,
the one of time, the other of identity. Of the two the basic one is the
exploitation of Virgil's Paganism for the purpose of "staging" the
triumph of Christianity. But this, too, involved a play with time, of
historical time: a going back to the time of Paganism, a going forward (in the Past) to the advent of Christianity, leading to a return
to the action of the narrative: the Pilgrim's progress in his journey
to God. Inevitably, then, the play with narrative time must be seen
as an artistic reflection of the play with historical time, brought into
focus by the shifts within Virgil's psychology.

V

In the Valley of the Princes

TO PASS from the description of the First to that of the Second Advent involves, above all, a shift of mood and tone. The first represented a unique event on which the fate of mankind depended; as re-enacted within the limits of one small part of the story of the *Divine Comedy,* and made to converge on the solitary vulnerable figures of Virgil and the Pilgrim, it was tensely dramatic, filled with the suspense of "whether-or-not." But in the re-enactment of the Second Advent, the daily coming of Christ into the hearts of men, presented for the benefit of souls whose salvation is assured, there can be no atmosphere of agonizing suspense. The dilemma of "whether-or-not" has been solved: all the sinners in Purgatory are saved, and they know that they are saved. In the Valley of the Princes, where the atmosphere is determined, not by the mood of the Pilgrim or of Virgil, but by that of the inhabitants themselves, this atmosphere is one of tranquillity, serenity and absolute confidence.

This does not mean that we should expect absence of the "theatrical"; since the representation of the Second Advent must, like that of the First, take us briefly outside the confines of the story, at the same time that it must be realized on a stage set up within these confines, the suggestion of "theater" cannot be avoided. But there will be no screaming demons, no hideous landscape, no thundering earthquakes. The background will be that of a *locus amoenus;* the

only sounds heard are the sweet melodies of a chorus chanting evening hymns, or the words of individual Christian souls engaged in
courteous conversation or serious exposition. (For a very brief moment there is heard the sound of angel's wings cleaving the air.) Of
course, the contrast between the mood of the First Advent and that
of the Second is mainly a contrast between the first and second can-
ticles of the *Divine Comedy,* between Hell and Purgatory: in the
Purgatory, after the initial bewilderment of the newly-arrived souls,
the atmosphere of serenity prevails throughout.

But the *Purgatory* offers another new element, and one that the
reader will recognize first—in fact, it is suggested already in the
final line of the *Inferno,* when the Pilgrim and his guide emerge
from the "cammino ascoso" that has led them from the depths of
Hell, and they see the stars; the reader has the sudden impression
of a return from the after-life to this world. And the first canto of
Purgatory begins (after the invocation of the Muses) with a description of the splendor of the heavens just before daybreak. It is
as if the first canticle had ended and the second had begun with the
Pilgrim's return to earth, to our world. And in every one of the first
eight cantos, that is, throughout the description of the ante-Purgatory, there will be a reference to the condition of the heavens, to the
play of sunlight and shadow, to the changing times of day. Several
of these indications are given in descriptions of consummate artistry.

All such references cease once the Pilgrim has passed through
the gate, for in Purgatory proper there is a changeless atmosphere
(a phenomenon discussed by Statius in Canto XXI). But the frequent reminders of atmospheric conditions to be found in the first
eight cantos would seem to indicate that Dante is presenting the
ante-Purgatory as an imitation of our world. And these particular
reminders of our world are surely intended to prepare us for the
"worldly" atmosphere, on different levels, that pervades the ante-
Purgatory, particularly the Valley of the Princes.

On the psychological plane what is first noted is the concern for
worldly things shown by the souls whom the Pilgrim encounters.
The first of those to appear in the ante-Purgatory is Casella whose

sin (like those of the other souls in the ante-Purgatory) we will
never know; he gladly agrees to sing one of Dante's love poems—to
which the entire group of his companions, including the Pilgrim
and Virgil, listen with rapt attention ("come a nessun toccasse altro
la mente" II, 117), until the concert of worldly music is harshly
interrupted by Cato:

> . . . "Che è ciò, spiriti lenti?
> Qual negligenza, quale stare è questo?
>   Correte al monte a spogliarvi lo scoglio
>   ch'esser non lascia a voi Dio manifesto!"   (II, 120–123)
>
> (. . . "What's going on here, lazy souls?
> What negligence, to stand around like this!
>   Run to the mountain, strip off all the filth
>   that keeps the sight of God away from you!")

Cato's harsh words to the newly-arrived souls should be remembered
when the reader comes to meet the other Penitents in the ante-
Purgatory: Manfred, concerned, if only briefly, with the disposition
of his body; Belacqua, continuing to enjoy the indolence which
characterized his life on earth; Cassero and Montefeltro, who give
vivid accounts of their violent deaths and the location of their
bodies; La Pia who must inform the Pilgrim of her birthplace and
her last abode, and of her disastrous marriage; Nino, bitter over the
inconstancy of his wife who has remarried; Conrad, who could not
take his eyes off the Pilgrim once he learned that this was a person
who might give him information about the regions of Italy he loved.

But it is Sordello who is the most intensely concerned with
earthly ties and earthly values. He enthusiastically embraces Virgil
before he knows his name, simply because they come from the same
city. When he asks his name and learns that his fellow-Mantuan is
none other than Vergilius Maro, his awe and reverence suggest that
there are for him no higher values than those of art and fame. Virgil,
in naming himself, had spoken of being condemned because of his
lack of faith, but Sordello ignores his words: it is not the great poet's

doom or the workings of Divine Justice which concern Sordello so much as Virgil's fame (which has given glory to his native Mantua). And no doubt it is because he considers the Pilgrim to have no such worldly distinction that he shows himself indifferent to his presence. Not once does Sordello address the Pilgrim directly; though bewildered when he hears the Pilgrim reveal the fact to Nino that he is still alive, he simply turns away toward Virgil—his attitude offering a decided contrast to the fascinated reaction of Nino and Conrad. And when the serpent comes it is to Virgil that Sordello points it out.

Nowhere is Sordello's concern for earthly matters so elaborately displayed as in his identification of the rulers for Virgil's benefit, a lengthy discourse which gives him the opportunity to discuss the past and present politics of Europe. But does Dante allow Sordello this opportunity to develop his concerns in order to indict him for his worldliness? Sordello's words ring with moral fervor! No, no indictment is intended: Sordello's description of the European scene is in the same vein, though less severe, as the even lengthier apostrophe of Dante the Poet which closes Canto VI ("Ahi serva Italia"). But the apparent inconsistency here involved is only apparent: the theme "concern for worldly things" which is found in every canto of the ante-Purgatory, from the moment the souls begin to appear (Canto II), is developed on different levels, from the most trivial to the most grandiose. And, as every reader of Dante knows, concern for human justice, the dream of the Empire, of the *beatitudo huius vitae* was indeed a grandiose concern, second only to the desire for the City of God, for the *beatitudo vitae eternae*. Cato was surely right in reprimanding harshly those who were so enraptured by Casella's popular music in Canto II, not because of the worldliness of their interest but because of the level on which this worldliness revealed itself. And Sordello *is* "concern for worldly things" incarnate, from the low level of snobbishness, to the eminence of his glowing words inspired by love of peace, justice and order. Because the desire for the *beatitudo huius vitae* is a noble one for Man living in this world, and because the ante-Purgatory is an imitation of this world, Sordello is allowed to express his feelings nobly. But, in

Purgatory proper the desire for the *beatitudo vitae eternae* alone prevails.

Not all is concern for worldly things in the ante-Purgatory. Most of the souls that the Pilgrim meets, from Manfred on, ask for the prayers of the living; and it is surely not worldliness that motivates the two groups that the Pilgrim hears singing psalms: *In exitu . . .* in Canto II and the *Miserere* in Canto V—though the second group do break off singing when they notice the shadow cast by the Pilgrim. But the most moving scene of piety is that of the group in the valley who sing two evening hymns as a prelude to the coming of the angels.

In spite of their piety, however, or rather, because of it—because of the particular form it takes—there are no characters in the ante-Purgatory who seem to be so much in and of this world as are those in the Valley of the Princes, who sing the *Salve regina* and the *Te lucis ante.* These hymns are intended to be sung at nightfall (this is expressly indicated in the opening words of the second hymn), a fact which immediately suggests the daily habits of a Christian community. And the words of the hymns themselves, expressing desires natural to Christians living in this world, are on the whole most inappropriate for the souls in the afterlife whose salvation is assured. The second hymn is a prayer to God that through Christ He may be their guardian against the Tempter:

> Te lucis ante terminum,
> rerum creator, poscimus
> ut solita clementia
> sis praesul ad custodiam.
>
> Procul recedant somnia
> et noctium fantasmata
> hostemque nostrum comprime
> ne polluantur corpora.
>
> Praesta, pater omnipotens,
> per Iesum Christum Dominum,

qui tecum in perpetuum
regnat cum sancto spiritu.

(Creator of all things,
before the end of light,
we beg you to guard and protect us
with your usual compassion.

Let the dreams and
fantasies of night retreat;
repress our enemy
lest our bodies be defiled.

Grant this, almighty Father,
through Jesus Christ the Lord
who rules with you
and the Holy Spirit forever.)

And, in fact, as the words of the hymn die away, the angels come.

But why should this group fear "our enemy"? They cannot sin; they cannot be tempted. Moreover, the central stanza of this hymn asks for protection against bad dreams; and the souls in the other world do not sleep and cannot dream. Only the Pilgrim will sleep that night (and have a terrifying dream), and Dante feels called upon to explain why his Pilgrim sleeps: because he, unlike the rest, was still burdened by "quel d' Adamo" (IX, 10).[1] This hymn must have been deliberately chosen because of its appropriateness for the condition of Christians living on earth. The reader is asked to forget that these souls are dead; we must see them as symbolizing all Christians in a state of grace.[2]

The first hymn, *Salve regina,* shows in a different way the same theologically "appropriate inappropriateness":

Salve, regina misericordiae,
vita, dulcedo et spes nostra, salve!
ad te suspiramus gementes et flentes.
Ad te clamamus exsules filii Evae,
in hoc lacrimarum valle.

Eia ergo, advocata nostra,
illos tuos misericordes oculos ad nos converte
et Iesum, benedictum fructum ventris tui,
nobis post hoc exsilium ostende,
o clemens, o pia
o dulcis Maria.

(Hail, Queen of mercy,
our life, sweetness and hope, hail!
moaning and crying, we sigh to you;
exiled children of Eve, we call to you
from this valley of tears.
Come, therefore, our Advocate,
turn those merciful eyes of yours on us
and reveal to us, after this exile,
Jesus the blessed fruit of your womb.
O merciful, O tender,
O sweet Mary.)

This is a prayer for salvation after death, expressing the sentiments of those still looking forward to death as the end of exile on earth. Not only do these souls in the Valley have no need to pray for salvation: it is also true that no prayer of their own for any manifestation of God's grace would have efficacy (that is why they show the Pilgrim such eagerness to be prayed for by the living). But, as has been said, this group is intended to symbolize the Christian community at prayer. And with the words *in hoc lacrimarum valle,* which occur soon after the singing begins, the focus is shifted from the splendid Valley of the Princes to "this vale of tears" on earth. It is as if the stage-director had instructed the singers once and for all that every day at sunset they should play the role of a pious Christian community. Thereby, the stage would be set for the coming of the angels; for the daily coming of Christ can take place only for Christians in this life.[3]

At the beginning of Canto VIII, after the *Salve regina* has come to an end, and just before the second hymn is begun, the poet introduces the haunting reference to the twilight hour when there is awakened, in the hearts of travellers who have just left home, a longing to see again the loved ones left behind: "Era già l' ora che volge il disio/ai navicanti. . . ." This tender image with its suggestion of exile, which seems to echo the mood of the hymn just sung, must be intended to convey the mood of the souls in the valley. But, if so, it would seem to imply a longing to return to the familiar scenes and loved ones left behind on earth. Could it be that the nostalgia of these souls is a blend of longing for this world and longing for Heaven? Perhaps we should understand that their longing for Heaven, as expressed in the hymn, is echoed here, in the image of the traveller, in terms of a longing for their earthly home—since up to the present it is the only home they have known. Perhaps, they are not quite used to being dead. (We are reminded of Rilke's words in the First of the *Duino Elegies:* "True, it is strange to inhabit the earth no longer. . . .") And until their penance actually starts, they can but dimly understand the significance of the stage they have reached beyond death.

Of the various groups of penitents in the ante-Purgatory, the ones in the Valley of the Princes are the only ones that seem to be at home there: the first four groups seem to belong nowhere. The first souls the Pilgrim sees, the newly-arrived, must ask directions of the two travellers. The group to which Manfred belongs, and the next group with Buonconte, seem to be wandering continuously, while the souls for which Belaqua is the spokesman happen to be resting at the moment in the shade of a great boulder, as if fatigued by their wanderings. But the Princes are assigned an abode and an atmosphere.

And their abode is one of sumptuous beauty:

> Oro e argento fine, cocco e biacca,
>   indaco legno lucido e sereno,
> fresco smeraldo in l'ora che si fiacca,
> da l'erba e da li fior dentr' a quel seno
> posti ciascun saria di color vinto,
>   come dal suo maggiore è vinto il meno.

Non avea pur natura ivi dipinto,
  ma di soavità di mille odori
  vi facea uno incognito e indistinto. (VII, 73–81)

(Gold and fine silver, cochineal and white lead,
  Indian wood, glowing, and deeply clear,
  emerald at the very instant it is split,
each of these would be surpassed in color
  by the grass and flowers set within that dale,
  as what is greater must surpass the lesser.
Not only had nature painted there, she also
  blended the sweetness of a thousand odors
  into one unknown, unrecognizable.)

Many commentators have suggested an easy comparison of this *locus amoenus* with that described in Canto XXVIII: the Earthly Paradise. But, for the background of the Princes, any suggestion whatsoever of "natural beauty" before the Fall of Man would be most unfitting; I should say that while an association of the two places was surely intended, this was only to point up the great contrast between the two. The beauty of the Earthly Paradise is a beauty that suggests the timeless and unchanging, and the purity that Nature once knew; it is a beauty meant to be absorbed and enjoyed by senses equally pure. The Pilgrim will make his way through the green forest surrounded by fragrance, the clean cool fragrance of verdant things; he feels the gentle breeze on his face and notes that it moves the branches that give a rustling accompaniment to the joyful songs of the birds in the treetops, as they greet the new day. The Pilgrim must stop as he comes to a stream of purest water which, with its little waves, moves the grass along its banks in harmony with its own movement (later, the sweetness of the water's taste will be mentioned). Beyond the river is a variety of flowering boughs and, gathering the colorful flowers and singing a psalm, a graceful maiden is to be seen. This is a delicate picture of world harmony, describing the home of Man before the Fall. And perhaps because of the innocence of the beauty of this place, it is described as appealing to all five senses.[4]

But in the description just quoted of the Valley of the Princes only two types of natural, sensuous phenomena are included: the visible and the olfactory. What was there to be seen was grass and flowers, but thanks to the list of metaphors (in the description of the Earthly Paradise nothing was compared to something it was not), what we are invited to visualize is precious metals, jewels (with the special glint that comes only at the moment they are split), dyes and pigments (raw materials for landscape painting), and the sheen of exotic wood, rich and dark and quietly luxurious. Nature, the Nature created by God, has given way completely to products of industry and the mechanic arts, man-made opulent beauty destined to perish, the only kind realizable after the Fall and loss of Eden.

In describing the fragrance of the flowers, the poet imagines that the sweetness of a thousand odors is blended into a single "unknown" odor. Gone is the smell of the rose, of the violet, of the lily, the essence of each being replaced by something it is not. If then, in the picture of the visible elements, natural beauty has been covered by layers of make-up—in the description of the fragrance which these give off, there has been a comparable camouflage: the disappearance of individual elements of natural beauty into something unrecognizable. This is the home of the Princes, this is the home of Mankind after the Fall, at its most luxurious. This is the background for the spectacle which takes place daily before the Princes, recalling the Fall while showing forth the possibility of Redemption.

The events that take place there begin with the meeting of the travellers and Sordello in Canto VI. Virgil, seeing a figure sitting off alone, stops to ask directions for the quickest way up the mountain (a number of times the Pilgrim's guide through Purgatory will have to ask directions, as he never had to do in Hell). When the stranger learns that Virgil is from Mantua, he embraces him and names himself. Canto VI ends with perhaps the most famous apostrophe in the *Divine Comedy:* a series of invectives beginning "Ahi serva Italia, di dolore ostello."

Canto VII consists, for the most part, of conversation, with Sordello as main speaker. Nothing happens except that he leads the two travellers to a point from which they can see in the valley below a group of souls sitting on the grass among the flowers, filling the perfumed air with the notes of an evening hymn, *Salve regina.* The canto concludes with Sordello's identification of the princes singing below.

In Canto VIII things quietly begin to happen (and the quietness of the tempo will continue throughout the canto). The group in the valley below begins another hymn, *Te lucis ante,* the reader at this point being invited by the poet to exercise his wits in interpreting what is about to happen. What happens is that two angels descend, who take up their posts on either side of the open valley. Between the advent of the angels and the arrival of the serpent two dialogues take place: Sordello has led the two travellers down into the Valley of the Princes, and the Pilgrim speaks first with his friend Nino Visconti, and then with Virgil (about the changed condition of the heavens). At this moment the serpent appears—to be quickly put to flight by the angels. The canto ends with a conversation between the Pilgrim and Conrad Malaspina.

Before attempting to analyze the mysterious events of Canto VIII, intended to represent the Second Advent, let us go back to where we began: the meeting in Canto VI between Virgil and Sordello, who will be the traveller's guide to the Valley of the Princes—assuming briefly, as it were, the role long played by Virgil. It is Virgil who first sees him and points him out to the Pilgrim as one sure to give them information:

> Ma vedi là un'anima che, posta
>   sola soletta, inverso noi riguarda;
>   quella ne 'nsegnerà la via più tosta." (VI, 58–60)

> (But see that spirit stationed over there,
>   all by himself, looking in our direction;
>   he will show us the quickest way to go.")

Then follows the description of Sordello:

> Venimmo a lei: o anima lombarda,
>   come ti stavi altera e disdegnosa
>   e nel mover de li occhi onesta e tarda!
> Ella non ci dicëa alcuna cosa,
>   ma lasciavane gir, solo sguardando
>   a guisa di leon quando si posa.
> Pur Virgilio si trasse a lei . . . (VI, 61–67)

> (We made our way toward him. O Lombard soul,
>   how stately and disdainful you appeared,
>   what calm and dignity was in your glance!
> He did not say a word to us, he just
>   let us keep moving up toward him, while he
>   was watching like a couchant lion on guard.
> Nevertheless, Virgil went up to him . . .)

And surely this description suggests the preeminence of Sordello's role. The disdainful dignity of his bearing is that of a leader, just as the comparison to a lion at rest suggests the regal; indeed, since Sordello may be called a Christian Virgil (though not on the same level as Statius), it is not impossible to see in the lion-image religious symbolism—perhaps the Lion of Judah.[5] And the extreme isolation of this soul ("anima . . . sola, soletta") from the rest of those who are yet to appear, also symbolizes his preeminence. Most of all, however, this is suggested by the way the description opens ("O anima lombarda"): for one moment there is heard the voice of Dante the Poet, who pauses to "remember" the effect made upon him by the first sight of Sordello. Here we have an interruption of the narrative, but one so smoothly executed that it is hardly noticeable, for the words which interrupt the narrative lead into the narrative again—since they begin the description of Sordello which the narrative then can easily continue. This device is used here to anticipate, lightly, the more explosive auctorial interruption that will take place later in the canto.

Virgil goes up to the silent figure who has been watching the two travellers approach, and asks him to show them the best way up the mountain. Instead of answering Virgil's question, however, the as-yet unidentified shade questions him, asking where the two are from, and about the conditions obtaining there. (The conversation between the Pilgrim and Conrad that brings Canto VIII to a close will begin with Conrad's request for information about conditions in Valdimagra.) At the word "Mantua," with which Virgil begins his answer, Sordello rushes toward him, to name himself and to embrace him.

> . . . e l'ombra, tutta in sè romita,
> surse ver' lui del loco ove pria stava,
>   dicendo: "O Mantoano, io son Sordello
>   de la tua terra!"; e l'un l'altro abbracciava. (VI, 72–75)

> (. . . and that shade, now no longer
> wrapped in himself, sprang to his feet, and ran
>   toward him: "O Mantuan, I am Sordello
>   of your own city." They embraced each other.)

Sordello's enthusiastic joy at meeting a fellow-townsman could not have been put into greater relief.

But hardly has the reader recovered from the suddenness of Sordello's interruption when there comes immediately a second interruption, on another plane; the last words of line 75 (". . . e l'un l'altro abbracciava") are immediately followed by:

> Ahi serva Italia, di dolore ostello,
>   nave sanza nocchiere . . . ! (VI, 76–77)

> (Ah, Italy enslaved, the abode of grief,
>   ship without a captain . . . !)

as the poet breaks off the narrative to launch into his series of invectives against Italy. Thus, the interruption that is part of the narrative (when Sordello prevents Virgil from finishing his sentence) is followed by an interruption of the narrative itself. The effect of both these impulsive interruptions is a heightening of emotional intensity: the first, that of Sordello's feelings for a newly-discovered fellow countryman, the second, that of the poet's feelings about the condition of his country—a condition so in contrast to the loving attitude of Sordello toward another Mantuan, whose name he does not even know.

But there has also been achieved another effect: the invective fills the rest of Canto VI (76–151), and Canto VII opens with Sordello still embracing Virgil:

> Poscia che l'accoglienze oneste e liete
>   furo iterate tre e quattro volte,
>   Sordel si trasse, e disse: "Voi chi siete?" (VII, 1–3)

> (When the joyous, ceremonious embrace
>   had been repeated three or four more times,
>   Sordello stepped away: "Who are you two?")

It is clear that the opening tercet of Canto VII could have followed immediately line 75 of Canto VI: ". . . e l'un l'altro abbracciava." Dante, instead, has interpolated between the first and final stages of Sordello's embrace the longest auctorial intervention in the whole of the *Divine Comedy,* interrupting narrative time with auctorial time (two shadowy figures are presented locked in an embrace, while a thunderous voice is heard reviling the Italian states). Now, it is true that whenever Dante pauses to speak in his own voice, this may be considered as an interruption of narrative time (in fact, there has just occurred a minor example of this: "O anima Lombarda . . ."); what sets this interpolation apart from all the rest, making the reader accutely aware of a shift in time, is not only its great length but the use of this device, for the only time in the *Divine Comedy,* to interrupt a brief, clear-cut act already in progress.

At the end of *Inferno VII,* two cantos before the coming of the *messo,* the poet had introduced a play with time to announce prematurely the arrival at "a tower"; here, in the last half of *Purgatory* VI, two cantos before the advent of the angels, he offers another variation of the same device. In this case, however, where time has been arrested, not speeded up surreptitiously, the impact of Dante's de-

vice is felt immediately. No one can read: ". . . e l'un l'altro abbracciava./Ahi serva Italia. . . !" and not feel the jolt!

Once the narrative is resumed and the embrace is concluded,
Sordello steps back slightly from the figure he had clasped in his
arms to ask his name. Virgil identifies himself, and adds the information that he has lost Heaven through no other sin than lack of faith.
Sordello's rapturous, incredulous joy, when he hears Virgil's name,
inspires him to embrace the Latin poet again (this time more rever-
ently), and to pour forth his praise. Then he asks Virgil whether
he comes from Hell and, if so, from what part. Obviously, he does
not realize that Virgil has already answered both his questions; when
Sordello heard "Io son Virgilio . . ." he must, out of pure joy, have
stopped listening to the important words that followed (VII, 7–8):
". . . e per null' altro rio/lo ciel perdei che per non aver fè." Virgil
patiently answers his question, this time in considerable detail, evoking, in haunting terms, the sad atmosphere of Limbo (where, we
remember, the pagan Virgil had once witnessed the First Advent):

> Luogo è là giù non tristo da martìri,
>   ma di tenebre solo, ove i lamenti
>   non suonan come guai, ma son sospiri.
> Quivi sto io coi pargoli innocenti
>   dai denti morsi de la morte avante
>   che fosser da l'umana colpa essenti;
> quivi sto io con quei che le tre sante
>   virtù non si vestiro, e sanza vizio
>   conobber l'altre e seguir tutte quante.   (VII, 28–36)

> (There is a place down there made sorrowful
>   not by torments but only by the shadows,
>   where laments are not the screams of pain, but sighs.
> And there I dwell along with innocent
>   infants seized by the teeth of death, before
>   they could be cleansed from the stain of original sin;
> And there I dwell with those who were not clothed
>   with the three holy virtues, but, unsinning,
>   knew all the rest and put them into practice.)

The reader may wonder why three tercets are devoted to a second description of Limbo, which was already vividly described in *Inferno* IV. But here the picture is presented from the point of view of Virgil himself, who is cut off from the vision of the God he had come to know too late. It is the note of exile that Virgil sounds, anticipating the mood of the first evening hymn, in which is concentrated the nostalgia of all the souls of the ante-Purgatory. And in fact, the ante-Purgatory itself is a Limbo—though, thanks to the grace of God, it is a temporary one. The reader must realize that if Sordello had listened more carefully to Virgil's words about himself, we would never have had this intimate picture of Limbo. Then he will understand why Sordello was not allowed to listen more carefully.

The new acquaintance tells the two travellers that their ascent of the mountain must wait until morning, and he suggests that they go with him to a resting place where certain souls are gathered together who will make pleasant company. Virgil and the Pilgrim, with Sordello as their guide, follow a slanting, gradually-ascending path until they are able to see below the Valley of the Princes.

When the Pilgrim on the slope first sees the home of the Princes, he also sees immediately the souls gathered there, singing. But the reader does not. The poet has arranged a slow coming-into-focus of the group below. First of all, the reader learns from Sordello of the nearby presence of certain souls, before these are presented to his view; and they will be presented only by degrees. What the reader sees in the lavish description quoted earlier is the beautiful grass and the flowers, and the odor which these exhale; only afterward are we told that there are people in the valley, and even then the souls are presented in slow motion:

> "Salve, regina" in sul verde e 'n su' fiori
> quindi seder cantando anime vidi,
> che per la valle non parean di fuori. (VII, 82–84)

> ("Salve, regina," on the grass and flowers
> from where I stood I saw souls sitting, singing,
> hidden till then beneath the valley's rim.)

First the sound of the hymn is heard, then the grass and flowers are mentioned again, before the reader is told of the souls who are sitting there as they sing—and who are characterized only in terms of their previous invisibility ("che per la valle non parean di fuori") : there is offered in their presentation no sensuous detail whatsoever that invites to visualization. It is only when Sordello begins to identify them, still standing above them on the slope, that we can see them—through Sordello's eyes. But then, thanks to Sordello, we see them more sharply, in greater detail, than we see any individuals grouped together anywhere else in the *Divine Comedy.* As he calls the name of each individual, commenting on his role in recent European history, Sordello points out some physical feature of his, or facial expression, or posture, or at least the place he occupies among his fellows. What is evoked is like a Renaissance painting of a group in which each member is individualized.[6]

As every commentator would point out, Sordello's presentation of the Princes in the Valley is based on Book VI of the *Aeneid,* in which Anchises in Elysium leads Aeneas to the top of a hillock and from there points out in the dell below certain illustrious souls that are fated to be reborn. But the parallel between the two passages involves also matters of detail; the roll-call of names beginning with that of Sylvius:

> Ille, vides? pura juvenis qui nititur hasta,
> proxima sorte tenet lucis loca ... (*Aeneid* VI, 760–1)
>
> (That youth you see there leaning on the headless spear
> holds by lot the place nearest the light ...)

includes also indications of the figures' location or posture, or bearing, or equipment. So the poet Dante has learned from Virgil the technique of clearly outlining individuals in a group, yet at the same time showing them as a group; and he illustrates this in a description which he gives to Sordello to address to Virgil—for it is to Virgil alone that Sordello speaks. There is irony in the fact that Anchises' picture of illustrious men who will perform great deeds in the fu-

ture, serving to create and expand the Roman Empire, should serve
as inspiration for Sordello's picture, involving figures many of
whom have failed as rulers, even contributing to the decay of the
Holy Roman Empire.

Dante follows the author of the *Aeneid* in allowing the group of
souls to be seen first through the eyes of the protagonist and, again,
as they are pointed out by his guide. In the Latin text this twofold
presentation had been accompanied by a shift of vantage point:
before the individuals in the crowd are identified and characterized
by Anchises from the hilltop, Aeneas has gotten his first blurred
view of them while still in the valley where they are. Dante does not
shift terrain (both descriptions present the view from the slope),
but he does achieve a twofold point of view in a much more subtle
and elaborate way, the dual presentation involving a dual symbolic
value. As first presented to the reader, whose view of them has been
deliberately delayed, the souls below appear as an undifferentiated
mass and, as such, they are meant to symbolize, as they pray to the
Virgin, all Christians in a state of grace who live in the valley of this
our world. Then, with Sordello's words, the mass is molded into
various shapes who represent, on the one hand, the rulers of Europe
necessarily concerned in their lifetime with worldly things; on the
other hand, they represent mankind not yet in a state of grace. For,
being reminded of their actions, that is, of their life on earth, the
reader is reminded of the fact (which he was allowed to "forget"
in the first presentation) that, in life, they were impenitent—until
the last minute. (And that rulers should represent humanity is quite
fitting, enjoying, as they do, greater opportunity for developing
their human potentialities for good or for evil). But, while Sordello
proceeds to present the princes in their worldly aspect, the reader is
not allowed to forget that, as humble Christians in a state of grace,
the group continues singing; in fact, it is Sordello who keps reminding us of this in his descriptions of the individual figures. Just how
the first hymn (of eleven lines) already begun before Sordello takes
over, could last throughout his speech (of forty-six lines) we do not

ask; the literal impossibility is simply a sign that the poet wills us to hear Sordello's words against the background of voices raised in prayer to God.[7]

And once Sordello has stopped speaking, the shapes blend again into an undifferentiated mass except for the one anonymous individual whom the Pilgrim now sees rise to direct the group in singing a second hymn. Being anonymous, he represents the mass of souls, as these represent repentant Christians in this world praying to God. Thus, to the twofold presentation of the souls in the Valley, there is added a third stage as an *aria da capo:* first, the undifferentiated hymn-singing group, then the outlines of individuals representing worldliness, then again the mass of souls (which, later, when the Pilgrim finally comes down into the valley, has somehow dissolved: he sees there only Nino and Conrad).

Sordello's identification of the Princes, as we know, brings Canto VII to a close. But has he stopped speaking in the final line (". . . fa pianger Monferrato e Canavese")? At the beginning of the next canto it becomes clear that the Pilgrim has not heard him through until the end, his attention having been distracted by a movement in the group of souls seated in the valley below him. One of the figures has risen and is signing with his hand to be heard; then, joining his palms, and as if communing with God (how carefully the Pilgrim is observing!), he begins to sing the evening hymn *Te lucis ante* whose sweet music enraptures the Pilgrim. The others join in, their eyes, too, fixed on the heavens until the hymn comes to an end. (It is at that moment that Dante speaks to his reader, asking him to sharpen his eyes to the truth which is now so thinly veiled.) Now silent, they continue to keep their eyes raised, as if in expectancy—until the angels come.

The prolongation of their expectancy gives way to a prolonged description of the arrival of the angels: from on high they descend with flaming swords, blunt-tipped; their garments of a tender green (the color of newborn leaves) float behind them, fanned by their green wings. They separate to alight: one on the bank of the valley close to the observers on the slope, the other on the opposite side. And the Pilgrim sees their flaxen hair, and is dazzled by the radiance of their countenances.

Then Sordello speaks and the spell is broken, in two stages. First comes his matter-of-fact, almost casual explanation of the miraculous event they have all just witnessed: both come from Mary's bosom to guard the valley because of the serpent who is soon to come (and the reader knows immediately that what he has just seen, is seen every day by the inhabitants of the valley). The Pilgrim trembles with fear, not knowing, so he tells us, from which direction the serpent will come. Then, like the courteous host he has shown himself to be, Sordello suggests that they descend to meet "the great shades" in the valley, who will be delighted to see them. It is as if nothing transcendental has happened and nothing more is expected to happen. The atmosphere of reverie and awe, so carefully and consciously created by the poet, is completely destroyed by Sordello, once and for all.

In spite of the darkness that now prevails, the Pilgrim is able to recognize his friend, Judge Nino—who, when he learns to his bewilderment how the Pilgrim has gained access to the ante-Purgatory, calls out to Conrad to come and see "what God has willed"; then, turning back to him, he begins to plead for his daughter's prayers and to rebuke his wife's inconstancy. It is during a conversation between Virgil and the Pilgrim about the presence of three new stars in the heavens that Sordello draws Virgil close and,. pointing his finger to a certain spot in the valley, announces: "Behold our adversary!" And the Pilgrim sees the serpent:

> Da quella parte onde non ha riparo
>   la picciola vallea, era una biscia,
>   forse qual diede ad Eva il cibo amaro.
> Tra l'erba e' fior venìa la mala striscia,
>   volgendo ad ora ad or la testa, e 'l dosso
>   leccando come bestia che si liscia. (VIII, 97–102)

(At the little valley's open side there was
   a snake; perhaps it was the very one
   that offered Eve the bitter fruit to eat.
Through grass and flowers slid the vicious streak,
   turning its head around from time to time
   to lick its back like a beast that sleeks itself.)

The drama initiated with the slow descent of the angels is brought to
a swift conclusion: before the Pilgrim is aware of it, the angels have
left their posts; there is the sound of green wings cleaving the air,
the serpent flees, the angels return to their posts:

Io non vidi, e però dicer non posso,
   come mosser li astor celestïali,
   ma vidi bene e l'uno e l'altro mosso.
Sentendo fender l'aere a le verdi ali,
   fuggì 'l serpente, e li angeli dier volta,
   suso a le poste rivolando iguali. (VIII, 103–108)

(I did not see so I cannot describe
   the heavenly falcon's first movement of flight,
   but I saw clearly both of them come flying.
At the sound of their green wings cleaving the air
   the serpent fled; and the angels wheeled around
   flying in perfect time back to their posts.)

At last, the shade who was summoned by Nino and who has been
staring at the Pilgrim ever since, decides to address him, asking for
news of Valdimagra or places close by.[8]
   That Dante has represented the Second Advent as he has offers
no difficulty: the daily coming of Christ into the hearts of Christians
to protect them against temptation, symbolized by the daily coming
of the angels to protect the valley from the serpent signifying the
Fall of Man. That this should be enacted only for the benefit of those
in the valley is also acceptable, given their exemplary status. But
what meaning could this spectacle have for them or for anyone in

Purgatory? Everyone there is saved and is forever free from temptation. And it is surely in recognition of this fact that the serpent is
presented as so harmless (licking itself as a kitten might), and the
angels' swords are blunted. It is true that, for us, the souls in the
valley are intended to represent Christians living in our world for
whom the danger of temptation is ever present; but they themselves
know that this danger is nonexistent for them.

One could imagine that, particularly for those souls who were
saved so late, it could be spiritually edifying to meditate on human
susceptibility to temptation and on the miracle of grace that purifies
man's heart. But it is impossible to believe that such edification was
the purpose of this daily spectacle, because of the total lack of interest shown by the inhabitants of the valley. Sordello's remarks about
the angels and the serpent are offered as a courtesy to his guests, and
they betray no emotion whatsoever. As for the other souls in the valley, there is no specific indication that they are aware of the presence
of the angels or have noticed the entrance of the serpent and his
defeat. Indeed, we know for a fact that one of the characters, Conrad, was not even interested enough to look at the final event, for
we are told that he did not remove his eyes from the Pilgrim once
Nino had called his attention to him.

In my earlier article on the Advents I suggested that this drama
was enacted not for the benefit of the inhabitants of the valley but
for the reader, for Everyman (represented by the Pilgrim), whom
the poet has just encouraged "to sharpen his eyes to the truth" of this
brilliant dumb-show. It is Everyman, I insisted, who must be reminded of the daily presence of temptation and of the possibility
of Christ's daily protection—not the group in the valley who know
they are among the elect destined ultimately for Heaven. But this
was a wrong interpretation, if for no other reason than the absurdity
of Dante's conceiving the continuous repetition of this daily event
only to allow the Pilgrim and the reader to witness it once. Moreover,
though none of the group shows any reaction to the spectacle once it
has begun, we must not forget those moments of expectancy at the

beginning of the canto when everyone had his eyes raised toward Heaven during the singing of the hymn and continued to look expectantly upward until the angels came.

No, they do not fear the serpent; they are not concerned about the outcome of the mock battle (this is surely made clear): they are incapable of being tempted, and for them the outcome of the battle between good and evil was already decided when they died. What did concern them (and we remember their total absorption in expectancy) was that important moment of the day when the angels would come as they had come before and would come again: a never-failing sign of God's grace, which means for them a reassuring reminder of their salvation. These are the late-repentant: on earth they had known only briefly assurance of salvation (had Guido da Montefeltro known even that?); here, in the ante-Purgatory, unlike those within the gates of Purgatory proper, they cannot be reminded of their salvation by the suffering of purgation.

But the Pilgrim (Everyman) fears the serpent. He is afraid because he does not know from what direction ("per qual calle") it will come. He is reacting "symbolically" as the Christian in this life, who must be on guard against temptation which may come from any direction. And the Pilgrim shows, in general, a remarkable sensitivity to what is happening. It is he who sees the soul in the valley arise to lead the evening hymn (Virgil is still listening to Sordello); he is enraptured by the sweetness of the singing; the detailed description of the descending angels must reveal how deeply his attention was absorbed; he is fascinated by the sight of the three new stars, and he is hungry for their meaning. (Later he will learn that they represent the theological virtues of Faith, Hope and Charity, and it is, of course, under their light alone that the drama of the Second Advent could be performed.) The contrast between the indifference shown by the souls in the valley to this drama, and the Pilgrim's avid interest in it, is the contrast between a soul that has been saved and a Christian still living in this world.

In staging the Second Advent Dante has reminded the reader

three times of the drama representing the First Advent by offering three contrasting parallels. As Virgil, in *Inferno* IX, was describing the city of Dis, the Pilgrim stopped listening to the words of his guide, for his gaze had been attracted to the top of the high tower where three figures had suddenly arisen. Here, in *Purgatory* VIII, the Pilgrim ceases to listen to Sordello, his attention attracted by one of the figures in the valley below who has risen to his feet.[9] There, the menacing and hideous spectacle of the three writhing Furies, frantic with rage; here, the calm gesture of a soul rising to invite his companions to join him in the evening hymn beseeching God's protection. Again, it is just after the notes of the hymn *Te lucis ante* have died away that Dante speaks to his reader, asking him to interpret well what is about to happen—which will begin with the silent descent of the angels. His words follow upon a period of narrative calm, and are followed by a period of calm. But in *Inferno* IX the address to the reader is inserted between two startling events: Virgil's movement of hysterical fear and the clap of thunderous noise announcing the coming of the *messo*.

Finally, the coming of the *messo* in *Inferno* IX and of the angels in *Purgatory* VIII is preceded by an atmosphere of suspense and expectancy. The closing lines of *Inferno* VIII announcing the imminent arrival of the *messo*, which seem to reveal a confident conviction of rescue, may remind the reader of the expectant attitude of the souls in the valley. But the confident mood of Virgil was short-lived, and the fears of the Pilgrim were never completely assuaged: before the *messo* comes, Virgil must try to reassure his ward three times and must struggle to reassure himself—before he is seized by panic at the sound of Medusa's name. In the scene in *Purgatory* VIII no words of reassurance are spoken, nor are they needed. With the hymn *Te lucis ante* sung by the souls who keep their eyes raised expectantly toward the heavens, and whose leader seemed to be communing with God, there is established a mood of confidence, absolute and tranquil. And it is into this atmosphere that the two angels, wearing the color of Hope, descend. In all three parallel pairs there is offered the contrast between excitement and calm, between fear and assurance.

When Beatrice came, Christ came. But before the Final Coming of Christ could be pre-enacted at the top of the Mountain of Purgatory, the *messo* had to come to the gates of Dis to re-enact the Harrowing of Hell, and the angels had to come to the Valley of the Princess to stage the daily miracle of the coming of grace into the hearts of all believers.

VI

The "Sweet New Style" That I Hear

IN ALL histories of Italian literature, as in all anthologies of Old Italian poetry whose writers are grouped according to schools, we find the label "dolce stil novo" applied to a way of writing love poetry practiced by certain poets around the time of Dante. Who were these poets? To many critics, the true "dolcestil-novisti" were Dante, his predecessor, Guido Guinizzelli, and his contemporary, Guido Cavalcanti (though Contini, for one, doubts whether Cavalcanti should be included); the majority would include along with these three all serious lyric poets who were Dante's contemporaries or immediate successors. And what is exactly the "dolce stil novo?" The definitions vary from critic to critic, ranging from a rather silly emphasis on pure effortless lyricism to a rather pedantic insistence on scholastic-philosophical tendencies.

Now the phrase "dolce stil novo," applied so often to the poetry of Dante and others, was, as we all know, coined by Dante himself and is to be found in *Purgatory* XXIV in the passage containing the conversation between the Pilgrim and a slightly earlier poet, Bonagiunta Orbicciani. At the beginning of Canto XXIV, while being guided through the terrace of the Gluttonous (for this canto, like the preceding one, deals with the sin of gluttony), the Pilgrim asks to have some of the more distinguished gluttons pointed out to him. His companion Forese names a number of them, beginning: "Questi"—and he points with his finger—"è Bonagiunta,/Bona-

giunta da Lucca." After the listing of names has ended, comes the
meeting between the Luccan poet and the Pilgrim, described in lines
34–63. The Pilgrim, interested by Bonagiunta's obvious interest in
him, and noting that he was murmuring something about "Gentucca" ("e non so che 'Gentucca' "), encourages him to speak up:

> Ma come fa chi guarda e poi s'apprezza
>   più d'un che d'altro, fei a quel da Lucca
>   che più parea di me aver contezza.
> El mormorava; e non so che "Gentucca"
>   sentiv' io là ov'el sentia la piaga
>   de la giustizia che sì li pilucca.
> "O anima," diss' io," che par sì vaga
>   di parlar meco, fa sì ch'io t'intenda,
>   e te e me col tuo parlare appaga." (XXIV, 34–42)

> (But just as one who observes then concentrates
>   on one more than another, I did with the one from Lucca,
>   who seemed more anxious than the rest to know me.
> He was mumbling; and something like "Gentucca"
>   I heard there where he felt the sore
>   of that justice that torments them so.
> "O soul" I said "who seems so very anxious
>   to speak with me, do so that I may understand you,
>   and with your speech satisfy both you and me.")

Bonagiunta offers a prophecy (the mysterious lady who one day will
be kind to Dante has never been identified) and then in the next
tercet asks a question:

> "Ma dì s'i' veggio qui colui che fore
>   trasse le nove rime, cominciando
>   'Donne ch'avete intelletto d'amore.' " (49–51)

> ("But tell me if I do not see that one
>   who brought forth the new rhymes, beginning
>   'Ladies who have intelligence in love.' ")

This question about authorship the Pilgrim does not answer, giving instead a description of his own poetic attitude:[1]

> E io a lui: "I' mi son un che quando
>   Amor mi spira, noto, e a quel modo
>   ch'e' ditta dentro vo significando." (52–54)

> (And I to him: "I am one who, when
>   Love breathes within me, takes note, and to that way
>   which he dictates within I give expression.")

In his response Bonagiunta confesses that he was unable to follow such a poetic procedure, as was true also of his two famous contemporaries, *Il notaro,* "the lawyer" (a name given often to Giacomo da Lentino, the inventor of the sonnet and the most distinguished representative of the Sicilian School) and Guittone d'Arezzo, representing the Pisan School, who composed some of the most elaborately intricate verse of Old Italian literature. And he seems to understand the reason for their failure to adopt such a poetic method:

> "O frate, issa vegg'io," diss' elli, "il nodo
>   che 'l Notaro e Guittone e me ritenne
>   di qua dal dolce stil novo ch'i' odo!
> Io veggio ben come le vostre penne
>   di retro al dittator sen vanno strette,
>   che de le nostre certo non avvenne;
> e qual più a gradire oltre si mette,
>   non vede più da l'uno a l'altro stilo."
>   E, quasi contentato, si tacette. (55–63)

> ("O brother, now I see," he said, "the fetter
>   that held the Notary and Guittone and myself
>   to one side of the sweet new style I hear!
> I see quite well just how your pens
>   follow closely behind the dictator,
>   which certainly was not the case with ours;

And no one who looks beyond sees better than I
the difference between one style and the other."
And, as one satisfied, he spoke no more.)

Moreover, according to the traditional interpretation of line 58
(*vostre penne* = "your pens") he applies Dante's description of his
method to other poets who, evidently, distinguish themselves, like
Dante, from the group represented by da Lentino, Guittone and
himself.[2]

Thus, the phrase "dolce stil novo" has been taken to apply first
to the maturer love poetry of the young Dante (the new rhymes beginning "Donne ch'avete intelletto d'amore"), then to the poetry
of others associated with him. As for what this phrase really denotes,
many scholars have attempted to expatiate on the Pilgrim's rather
vague summary ("I' mi son un che . . ."), then to use their formulas
in order to determine the entrance requirements to the school of the
"dolcestilnovisti."

But before I offer my own definition of the *dolce stil novo,* what
it is and who the practitioners of it were, let us study much more
carefully the famous conversation between Dante and Bonagiunta
in which the expression in question was born, and also attempt to
place our passage within a larger framework. For though this passage has been the object of much scholarly analysis, there are a number of striking, even puzzling details that have been overlooked or
treated insufficiently by the critics. Most important is the relationship
between Bonagiunta and the Pilgrim as partners in a conversation.
Why, for example, does Bonagiunta begin by mumbling ("El mor-
morava . . .")? And when he is asked to speak more clearly (". . . fa
sì ch'io t'intenda"), Bonagiunta (though, no doubt, enunciating
clearly) immediately utters an oracular statement that the Pilgrim
could not possibly understand. After concluding his prophecy, Bonagiunta asks a question, which the Pilgrim answers in a most indirect
manner—and which was quite superfluous: if Bonagiunta could
prophesy about Dante's future, and recognize in him the author of
"Donne ch'avete intelletto d'amore" he must have already known

who he was. Finally, we may note the special eagerness of Bonagiunta to speak with this visitor on his terrace and his great content-
ment when he had finished.

Again, what is the connection between Bonagiunta's prophecy
and the discussion of. the "dolce stil novo"? It is difficult to believe
that in this relatively short conversation Dante the Poet would introduce two topics with no connection whatsover. And why does
Dante, when introducing the mumbling Bonagiunta to the reader,
stress in such gruesome detail the lips from which the word
"Gentucca" issued? Only in order to remind us that his (gluttonous)
lips are being punished? Again, if the phrase *dolce stil novo* refers
to Dante's lyric poetry, how can Bonagiunta say that he is hearing
it at the moment (". . . the sweet new style *that I hear"*)? And
what is the "nodo" that he says prevented him and his two fellow-
poets from reaching the goal achieved by Dante? This is not speci-
fied in the passage. Finally, after Dante the Pilgrim-Poet has
described his own poetic procedure, why does Bonagiunta, without
transition, apply this to an unnamed group of poets?

Let us begin with the problem of the apparent lack of thematic
unity in our passage—a feature which, apparently, has disturbed
none of the commentators. But while no real effort has been made
to find out how the figure of the kindly Gentucca fits into the pattern
of our passage, which is otherwise concerned with poetic theory, it
is true that certain commentators have pointed out that she is one of
three virtuous ladies whose names are mentioned in the two cantos
dealing with the sin of gluttony, the others being Piccarda, the
saintly sister of Forese (Canto XXIV) and Nella, his pure and pious
wife (Canto XXIII).[3] But none has spoken exactly in terms of
"praise of a virtuous lady" as a theme thrice developed in our two
cantos. And to see in this a *theme,* in fact a potential literary theme,
is to see immediately the connection between Bonagiunta's words
praising Gentucca and the lines that immediately follow:

> "Ma dì s'i' veggio qui colui che fore
>   trasse le nove rime, cominciando
>   'Donne ch'avete intelletto d'amore.' " (49–51)

For in line 51 Bonagiunta is quoting the opening words of a poem of Dante's, the first canzone in the *Vita nuova,* whose theme is precisely praise of a virtuous lady: of the Lady Beatrice, desired by the angels in Heaven but allowed by God to remain awhile longer on earth, for the sake of him who loves and praises her, and to the end that her presence among others may purify the vile and bless the worthy.[4]

Now, in describing the beginning of Bonagiunta's praise of Gentucca, Dante, as we have noted, took pains to remind us of the lips which uttered the praise (and which had been the instruments of Bonagiunta's sin). If we turn to the previous canto, we see that the first indication given the Pilgrim of the presence of the Gluttonous is the sound of their voices (XXIII, 11) singing the opening words of the *Miserere:* "Labia mea, Domine [aperies, et os meum annuntiabit laudem tuam]:" that is, words which express the penitents' desire to use their lips in praise of God, those lips that once they had misused for sensual self-gratification. Thus, the cantos dealing with gluttony, which contain the theme of praise of a virtuous lady, open with the theme of praise of God. Surely, then, the former theme is intended to be a reflection of the latter, and the tortured lips of Bonagiunta are intended to recall the "Labia mea, Domine" of the *Miserere.*

Let us turn next to the difficulty represented by Bonagiunta's words ". . . dal dolce stil novo *ch'i' odo.*" Though it has been assumed as self-evident that "dolce stil novo" refers to Dante's lyrical poetry, such an assumption is, at least on the literal plane, preposterous: Bonagiunta is not listening to a reading of Dante's poetry at the moment! What he hears (i.e. has just heard) are the words of Dante describing his own poetic method; it must be these words, "I' mi son un, che . . . ," still ringing in his ears, that he calls the "dolce stil novo."[5]

And that the clause ". . . ch'i' odo" of this passage is intended to evoke an acoustic phenomenon is surely suggested by the parallel offered in the passage just discussed, containing the opening lines of the *Miserere:* when the Pilgrim hears the penitents chanting "Labia mea, Domine," he asks of Virgil, "O dolce padre, che è quel *ch'i' odo?*" (XXIII, 13). This suggestion is corroborated by a further parallel, occurring earlier: when, at the beginning of Canto XVI, the Pilgrim hears the voices of the Wrathful singing the prayer, "Agnus Dei . . . ," he asks, "Quei sono spirti, maestro, *ch'i' odo?*" (XVI, 22). In all three cases we are meant to sense the effect of sublime words on an impressionable listener.[6] Twice the words come from afar; they are the opening words of a hymn and they come, as music, to the ears of the Pilgrim. In our passage, however, they are addressed directly to an interlocutor: it is Bonagiunta who listens, enraptured (the Pilgrim's words are followed by Bonagiunta's exclamation: "O frate . . ."), to the voice of a poet who speaks of Love—which is the unifying theme of the *Divine Comedy.*

If, then, the phrase *dolce stil novo* applies only to the Pilgrim's words that Bonagiunta has just heard, these words must be studied still more in detail. First of all, they must be seen in the context of this canto, that is, as an answer to the (quite superfluous) question of Bonagiunta[7] who, with the words "Ma dì s'i' veggio qui colui che . . ." turns abruptly from consideration of a private event in Dante's personal (future) life to address himself to the historic figure of Dante as poet; and we may note the formality, the suggestion of distance in the epithet applied to Dante, "colui che . . ." (a distance which is increased by the preceding words, "Ma dì s'i' veggio qui . . ." instead of, e.g. "Ma dì se tu sei . . ."); and the same impersonal tone is continued in the Pilgrim's reply: the "colui che . . ." of Bonagiunta is echoed by "I' mi son *un, che* . . ." Since the Pilgrim knew that Bonagiunta had recognized him as Dante, there was, of course, no need for him to give a yes-or-no answer to his question; but what is exactly the relationship between this question and the answer that the Pilgrim chose to give? Now, though Bonagiunta speaks in general terms of "le nove rime," it seems clear that he recognized the particular significance of the first canzone of the *Vita nuova;* accordingly, Dante, though he gives a general description of his "poetic method," must intend his words to have a special reference to the composition of this canzone. What this reference is can be seen only by turning to the *Vita nuova:* Dante's words must be seen not only in the context of this canto, but also in that of his "autobiographical" poem.

Dante's sense of a man's need to develop from self-centeredness and self-pity to selflessness is described in the *Vita nuova* not only in the poems but also in the prose narrative. Less conspicuous is an earlier development that must have taken place, resulting in the sublimation of his protagonist's sensuous desires. In spite of the fact that there is no reference in the first part of the work to sensuous longings, we must suppose that these existed because of the vision Dante describes in Chapter III; in fact, the semi-nude female figure in Love's arms is twice described, the more detailed description being given in the preceding prose passage, which obviously we are meant to have in mind as we read the more discreet version in the poem. The opening sonnet of the *Vita nuova* is surely one of the most erotic love lyrics of the courtly poetry of the *duecento*.

The opening part of the *Vita nuova,* containing the first ten poetic compositions, is mainly concerned with the poet's emotional experiences (his hopes, his fears, his sufferings—his deepest suffering having been caused by Beatrice's refusal to greet him); then, in Chapter XVII, the young Dante resolves never again to write about his longing for Beatrice and to choose instead, "matera nuova e più nobile che la passata." In the next chapter he tells (that is, he reports the words he uttered to a group of gracious ladies) what that choice was and how it came about:

> "Madonne, lo fine del mio amore fu già il saluto di questa donna, di cui voi forse intendete; ed in quella donna, dimorava la mia beatitudine, che era fine di tutti i miei desiderii. Ma poichè le piacque di negarlo a me, lo mio signore Amore, la sua mercede, ha posta tutta la mia beatitudine in quello che non puote venir meno . . . in quelle parole che lodano la donna mia." (Chapter XVIII)

> ("Ladies, the end and aim of my love formerly lay in the greeting of this lady to whom you are perhaps referring, and in this

greeting dwelt my bliss which was the end of all my desires.
But since it pleased her to deny it to me, my lord, Love, through
his grace, has placed all my bliss in something that can not fail
me . . . in those words that praise my lady.")

Once earlier Dante's lord, Love, had dictated to him the theme of a
love poem: on that occasion, a poem intended to seek the forgiveness
of Beatrice. Now he is told by Love that not only his poetry but his
thoughts and feelings must take a new direction; he must find his
happiness not in what he can obtain from his lady but in what he
can give her: words of praise. At this point in the *Vita nuova* Dante
had learned the beauty of loving unselfishly, that is, purely;[8] it is
surely that moment in his spiritual development when Love breathed
within him and he took note (the poetic result being "Donne
ch'avete intelletto d'amore") that Dante has in mind when he says
to Bonagiunta,

> . . . "I' mi son un che, quando
> Amor mi spira, noto, e a quel modo
> Ch'e' ditta dentro, vo significando."

And, if at the much further stage of development he has reached in
Canto XXIV of the *Purgatory,* the Pilgrim still declares himself to
be in absolute, unqualified subjection to Love, we must remember
that he has been thoroughly indoctrinated by Virgil (*Purgatory*
XVIII) on the subject of love,[9] that is, the different kinds of love,
with the necessary restrictions and qualifications, and that there is
no danger of his believing "ciascun amore in sè laudabil cosa"
(XVIII,36). For him, henceforth, Love is "l'Amor che move il
sole e l'altre stelle." And as Dante allowed the poet-pilgrim in the
Divine Comedy to compose his *credo* ("I' mi son un che . . ."),
he knew that it was Love who had inspired him to write also this
work; again, Love must have suggested "matera più nobile che la
passata."[10]

Thus the phrase "dolce stil novo" instead of referring to a body
of poetry refers to Dante's words about his poetic method, which is,

first of all, the expression of an attitude toward Love—an attitude which allowed for spiritual growth according as he came to understand more and more fully the ultimate meaning of Love.

Next, let us consider the *nodo* which Bonagiunta mentions (55) but does not define; nor do the commentators offer an explicit definition of it. Probably the answer seemed obvious to them: so long as "dolce stil novo" was considered to refer to Dante's "nove rime," the *nodo* which prevented Bonagiunta and the other two poets from matching Dante's poetry would be simply their failure to follow his method ("I' mi son un che . . ."); but since the phrase refers to words that Bonagiunta has just heard (the description of Dante's poetic method) such a vague and negative interpretation of *nodo* is impossible. There must have been a positive, specific "thing" which prevented Bonagiunta (and, in his opinion, also the other two poets he mentions) from following Dante's method.

And what this may have been, I believe, is suggested by a comparison, once again, of our passage with the two others just cited containing *ch'i' odo:* in both, just as in our passage, the verb is in rhyme with *nodo:*

> "O dolce padre, che è quel ch'i' odo?"
> comincia' io; ed elli: "ombre che vanno
> forse di lor dover solvendo il nodo." (XXIII, 13–15)

> ("O sweet Father what is that I hear?"
> I began. And he: "Shades that go
> loosing, perhaps, the knot of what they owe.")

> "Quei sono spirti, maestro, ch'i' odo?"
> diss' io. Ed elli a me: "Tu vero apprendi,
> e d'iracundia van solvendo il nodo." (XVI, 22–24)

> ("Are these spirits, master, that I hear?"
> I said. And he answered me: "You judge right,
> and they are loosing the knot of anger.")

In both cases, obviously, the "knot" in question that must be loosened is the sin being atoned for in Purgatory, and I believe, given the parallelism just indicated, that the same interpretation holds for the *nodo* of our passage (55). If so, the "knot" that Bonagiunta laments is the sin of gluttony—if this is taken in a larger sense as the vice of utter self-centeredness and greediness, the vice that the young Dante had suffered from in the selfish stages of his love for Beatrice in the *Vita nuova.*

And, similarly, Bonagiunta, during the time spent on the terrace of the Gluttonous, has come to see that his former inability to transcend completely his desires for the pleasures of this world, that his self-centered conception of happiness and of love was detrimental also to his art; his poetry, he realizes (like that of da Lentino and Guittone), is inferior to that of Dante's "nove rime" which at last he has come to understand and appreciate.[11] To the one who through his poetry had helped him in his development he wishes to reveal the stage of spiritual growth he has thus far attained.[12] And he believes that this will be made clear to the Pilgrim by means of his simple, objective, respectful question:

> "Ma dì s'i' veggio qui colui che fore
>   trasse le nove rime, cominciando
>   'Donne ch'avete intelletto d'amore.' " (49–51)

That Dante did understand is suggested by the nature of his intimately personal reply "I mi son un che. . . ."

But Bonagiunta had wished to do something more, as we have seen, to make some attempt to put into practice the lesson he had learned from Dante. And so, at first timidly, he had murmured the name of the lady he would unselfishly praise; then, encouraged by Dante's warm invitation to continue, he lost all diffidence and proceeded to make the prediction that would redound to the glory of the generous lady who was to succor the poet in his exile and redeem the reputation of Bonagiunta's native city of Lucca. His act of praising a generous deed from which he himself could derive no profit was a modest achievement, to be sure, in comparison with that of the other poet whom he addressed, but one can hardly compare to a

finished artistic production what must have been an improvisation
inspired by Dante's miraculous appearance on the terrace.[13] Given,
then, his desire to demonstrate to Dante (in two different ways) the
stage of spiritual-poetic development he had reached as a by-product
of "solvendo il suo nodo," we now understand his great satisfaction
once he had finished: "E, quasi contentato, si tacette."

And now we come to the nonsequitur represented by the "your
pens" of line 58, for a nonsequitur it surely is! In lines 52–54 Dante
describes his method of literary composition, which is based on his
responsive attitude to Love's dictation; and he emphasizes that this
method is intended to apply to himself alone by the very personal
tone he gives to the opening words "I' mi son un che. . . ." Yet
Bonagiunta, whose reply seems to bespeak complete understanding,
takes up Dante's description of his personal poetic experience only
to paraphrase it in such a way that it seems to apply to a group of
poets, a group whose existence has not been in question and whose
members he does not identify: "Io veggio ben come le vostre penne
/ di retro al dittator sen vanno strette. . . ." That Bonagiunta is interested in Dante's own way of writing poetry is clear from the fact
that he sees the poet as the author of "[. . . le nove rime, comin-
ciando] 'Donne ch'avete intelletto d'amore.' " For in this canzone,
as we have seen, Dante has described a type of love new in his personal experience and hardly known to any of his contemporaries.
Why, then, this sudden reference to "le vostre penne," which is
interpreted by all the translators I have consulted as "your pens"
(i.e. "your pen and those of others")?[14]

I believe that this is not the correct interpretation of "vostre
penne" and not only because of the nonsequitur it would involve:
even if there had been question of a group of poets before, there is
at least one grave objection to the traditional interpretation of
". . . le vostre penne . . .": the image suggested, if we attempt to
visualize it, is fuzzy, weird and ridiculous. A few (?) pens, held in
invisible (?) hands, writing and at the same time moving forward
behind the being who is dictating to them, and who must either be

moving in reverse, or else has his back turned on them as he dictates and moves ahead.[15]

All difficulties disappear if we translate *penne* not as 'pens' but as 'wings,' and see in the pronoun *vostre* the honorific replacement of *tue*. The interpretation *vostre penne* = 'your (thy) wings' is surely acceptable: though *penna* 'pen' occurs in the *Divine Comedy,* the plural *penne,* in all its other seventeen occurrences, has an anatomical reference;[16] and the use of the second person plural as an expression of respect toward an individual needs no justification in Old Romance literature. As for its use in the *Divine Comedy,* the honorific plural appears twice in the same canto (*Purgatory,* XXVI) —both times in an exchange between poets. When Guinizzelli asks Dante (using the second person singular) the reason for the affectionate attitude he shows him:

> "... *dimmi,* che è cagion per che *dimostri*
> nel dir e nel guardar avermi caro?" **(XXVI, 110–111)**

> ("... tell me, for what reason do you show yourself,
> by what you say and how you look, to hold me dear?")

he is answered: "... Li dolci detti *vostri* ..." **(XXVI, 112)**. Toward the end of the same canto when the Pilgrim turns to the shade who was pointed out by Guinizzelli as ". . . miglior fabbro del parlar materno" **(XXVI, 117)** and delicately suggests a desire to learn his name,[17] Arnault Daniel replies:

> "Tan m'abellis *vostre* cortes deman,
> qu'ieu no me puesc ni voill a vos cobrire...." **(XXVI, 140–141)**

(Here we have a most paradoxical hierarchy suggested by the use of the honorific pronoun. The pilgrim-poet addressed by Guinizzelli as *tu* in turn addresses him as *voi;* Guinizzelli having been elevated to a superior position by Dante points to a figure superior to himself who brings the circle full round by elevating Dante above himself.)

It is true that Bonagiunta's use of *voi* to Dante represents a shift
in his mode of address: he had first (**XXIV**, 84) used *tu* (". . . che
ti farà piacere"), repeating this form of address for several lines
more.[18] Only in line 58 does *voi* appear. But the shift from *tu* to *voi*
(also characteristic of Old Romance) is not lacking in the *Divine
Comedy:* several cantos earlier (*Purgatory,* XIX, 91–96), the Pilgrim had addressed as "tu" an unknown being lying prostrate before him, whose identity he wished to know; and when Pope Adrian
finished speaking, the Pilgrim was already kneeling; to the Pontiff's
amazed question "Qual cagion . . . in giù così ti porse?" he answers:
"Per *vostra* dignitate. . . ." There, the "*voi* of respect" was a reaction
to a revelation of identity; in our canto, what suddenly prompts the
Luccan poet to address the figure before him as "voi" is the sub-
limity of the words just uttered ("I' mi son un che . . ."). Thus, in
the lines "Io veggio ben come le vostre penne / di retro al dittator
sen vanno strette . . ," Bonagiunta is re-affirming Dante's self-
description, introducing a new image: that of wingèd flight guided
by Love, the "dittator."

And if *le vostre penne* is an allusion to the "wings" of Dante,
if, that is, Bonagiunta's remarks are concerned only with the single
poet Dante, then all the scholarly speculation about the individual
members of the group supposedly referred to in line 58 turns out
to be nonsensical—as does also the name with which they have been
baptized: the agèd label *dolce stilnovisti* has been coined as a result
of complete misunderstanding of Bonagiunta's words.

Thus, with the new interpretation of *le vostre penne* here proposed, there has not only been eliminated the rather ludicrous consequences for literary scholarship of the traditional one: we are also
rewarded by a poetic image (the wingèd flight of a soul guided by
Love) more illuminating than that of busy pens.[19] In fact, with the
correct interpretation of Bonagiunta's words there is offered a
broader poetic perspective for viewing the entire passage in question. In the light of the new image, the *nodo* of line 55 can be seen
as a fetter of some sort that would restrain a soul from upward flight;
we can sense better now the emphasis on the spatial involved in

". . . *di qua dal* dolce stil novo. . . ." And now too we understand the simile of the birds which follows our passage:

> Come 'li augei che vernan lungo 'l Nilo
>   alcuna volta in aere fanno schiera,
>   poi volan più a fretta e vanno in filo,
> così tutta la gente che lì era . . . (64–67)

> (As birds that pass the winter on the Nile
>   will sometimes flock together in the air
>   and then go single file and fly much faster
> just so it was with all the people there . . .)

After the lull, which hardly has duration, of Bonagiunta's silence ("e quasi contentato si tacette"), comes the effect of rushing wings.

And the new perspective gained is not even limited to our canto: the image that Bonagiunta offers of Dante's wings moving "di retro al dittator" finds counterparts throughout the *Purgatory* and *Paradise* (as only a superficial glance at the *Dante Concordance* reveals; cf. *penne, piume, ali*). Already at the beginning of the Pilgrim's painful ascent of the Mountain of Purgatory on his way toward Beatrice, under the guidance of Virgil, this movement is described in terms of upward flight (indeed, progress on foot is declared to be impossible):

> Vassi in Sanleo e discendesi in Noli,
>   montasi su Bismantova in cacume
>   con esso i piè; ma qui convien ch'om voli;
> dico con l'ale snelle e con le piume
>   del gran disio, di retro a quel condotto
>   che speranza mi dava e facea lume. (IV, 25–30)

> (Go to San Leo, or go down to Noli,
>   climb to the top of Mount Bismantova,
>   on your two feet, but here a man must fly;
> yes, fly—with the swift wings of deep desire
>   and always following behind that Guide
>   who gave me hope, spreading his light before me.)

And much later, as the Pilgrim is nearing the top of the Mountain of Purgatory for his meeting with Beatrice (which Virgil has just promised him), we find the words:

> Tanto voler sopra voler mi venne
> de l'esser sù, ch'ad ogne passo poi
> al volo mi sentia crescer le penne. (XXVII, 121–23)

> (Such great desire upon desire came to me
> to be up there, that then with every step
> I felt my wings expanding for the flight.)

Four cantos later, during the meeting, when Beatrice reminds him of his inconstancy after her death, she reproaches him for his failure to fly upward toward her:

> Ben ti dovevi, per lo primo strale
> de le cose fallaci, levar suso
> di retro a me che non era più tale.
> Non ti dovea gravar le penne in giuso ... (XXXI, 55–58)

> (You certainly should have, after the first
> shaft of deceptive things, risen upward,
> following me who was no longer such.
> You should not have bent your wings toward the ground. . . .)

In *Paradise* XV Cacciaguida expresses his happiness over his kinsman's arrival ". . . mercè di colei / ch' all' alto volo ti vestì le penne / delle mie ali a così alto volo . . ." (cf. also *Par.* XXXII, 145–48).[20]

Now the reader may wonder: "Is there not a great difference between these five images and that of Bonagiunta?" For all but one of them (*Purg.* XXXI) refer to Dante the Pilgrim on his journey toward Beatrice in the other world (and all of them refer to his moral development in love), while Bonagiunta was referring to Dante as poet, describing the soaring flight of his poetic imagination inspired by Love. Was he, perhaps, describing more than he knew —or, did he know? Was he able to sense not only the uniqueness of the young poet's "new rhymes" but the stage reached by the Pilgrim in his spiritual development? When he said ". . . Io veggio ben come le vostre penne . . ," did he see that the initiation of upward flight announced in "Donne ch'avete . . ." was to lead to the complete spiritualization of love, becoming indistinguishable from perfect love of God? There is absolutely no doubt that he saw this.

In order to understand how this could be let us think back a moment to the first topic treated in this chapter: the praise of virtuous ladies. Only three ladies were named at the time, but there is a fourth mentioned at the end of Canto XXIII: the Pilgrim, speaking to Forese (a companion of his youth with whom he had exchanged verses of a frivolous and even obscene nature), brings in the name of Beatrice. Now, during the entire conversation between the Pilgrim and Forese, the shades of the Gluttonous, showing great curiosity about the strangeness of the visitor on their terrace (a man of flesh and blood!) had hovered close around them, stopping when they stopped, walking with them when they went ahead. It is clear from the text that they must have been listening to the visitor's conversation with Forese; and Bonagiunta, for one, when he heard the Pilgrim name Beatrice, must have known instantly that the strange visitor was Dante, whose lyric poetry was so familiar to him, particularly the beautiful "Donne ch'avete intelletto d'amore" written in praise of Beatrice.[21]

But he heard from the Pilgrim more than just the name of Beatrice: he heard about his dissolute poetic period spent with Forese, and then the story of his moral development beginning with his entrance into the "Dark Woods" (Canto I of the *Inferno*); then about his passage through the realm of the "truly dead," his journey up and around the Mountain of Purgatory "which straightens those whom the world made crooked"—until the present moment, and beyond to Beatrice. This is one of those rare instances in the *Divine Comedy* when Dante the Pilgrim describes the plan of his entire journey into the Other World. And it is very strange that not a single commentator on Canto XXIV has seen what a privileged experience Bonagiunta had been granted before he actually began his conversation with the Florentine poet.

No wonder Bonagiunta was so eager to speak to the visitor on his terrace. No wonder he dared not address him directly and could only begin by murmuring. No wonder he still had to ask the incredulous question: "But tell me if I am *really* in the presence of the one who. . . ." No wonder he could speak of the Pilgrim's wings, of his flight (of his journey to Beatrice and to God).

The Pilgrim's wings were unfettered by the *nodo* that had held Bonagiunta back—the sin of gluttony, in the larger, in the poetic sense of this sin. For what greater contrast to the "wingèd flight behind Love" can be found than indulgence in gluttony? Movement forward, upward, away from the things of this earth as opposed to the act of filling oneself, making oneself heavy with the things of this earth. Gluttony is a taking into oneself, for oneself, a glorification of self. The wingèd flight is an escape from self into Love—a falling up into Love. And that Love and Gluttony represent not only two opposed attitudes but two opposed movements is brought out clearly at the very beginning of Canto XXIII: we remember the "Labia mea, Domine, aperies, et os meum annuntiabit laudem tuam . . ." sung by all the gluttons—the lips that they had used for taking into themselves, they now use (or pray to be able to use) in uttering, in sending forth, praise of God.[22]

Notes

I: A Lesson in Lust

1. I know of three scholars who have made a serious attempt to consider Canto V as a whole: Lanfranco Caretti (*Il Canto V dell' "Inferno,"* Firenze, 1967), Renato Poggioli ("Paolo and Francesca: Tragedy or Romance?", *PMLA*, LXXII [June, 1957]) and Irma Brandeis (*A Ladder of Vision*, London, 1960). Of these Caretti's treatment is by far the most detailed and the most penetrating.

2. Michele Barbi (*Dante*, Firenze, 1952) succeeds in fusing the Poet and Pilgrim so completely that he is utterly baffled (p. 186) by certain scholars who would, for example, deny that Dante felt pity for the two lovers: "non vedo," he says, "come si possa negare che Dante sente pietà dei due cognati e particolarmente di Francesca. Non bastano le parole,

..."Francesca, i tuoi martiri
A lacrimar mi fanno tristo e pio ..."

non basta che il poeta cada come morto *davanti ai piedi* dei due cognati, che *di tristizia* l'aveva tutto confuso?" Several noteworthy exceptions to this tendency are the studies of Lanfranco Caretti (*Il Canto V*) ; Irma Brandeis (*A Ladder*) ; Rocco Montano (*Storia della poesia di Dante I*, 1962, pp.399–413).

3. We shall, of course, never see Minos again, but in Canto XX, 35-36, we are reminded, in passing, of his presence at the entrance of Hell and of his function there; in Canto XXVIII, 124-127, he is described in more grotesque detail by Guido da Montefeltro, for whom the tail was coiled eight times around the enraged monster's body.

4. That the activities of Minos here described could not have been seen by the Pilgrim should be obvious. The brief interval between Minos' perception of the intruders and his suspension of activity would have allowed only the barest glimpse of the monster at work; but even if the Pilgrim had been able to examine him at his leisure, what he might have

seen would not have been described in the terms here offered us. If he had the time, he might have seen, for example, Minos wrap his tail around himself three times, and seen also the sinner standing before him plunge below. Next, eight times; next, four times, etc., etc., etc. But, depending on his senses alone, he would have failed to take in the significance of what he saw; surely he could not have "seen" what is described in lines 7–12 (note the *dico*):

> Dico che quando l'anima mal nata
> li vien dinanzi, tutta si confessa;
> e quel conoscitor de le peccata
> vede qual luogo d'inferno è da essa;
> cignesi con la coda *tante volte*
> *quantunque gradi* vuol che giù sia messa.

There is not a single detail in this description that invites to momentary visualization; and in every line it is made clear that the activity described is of a habitual nature and that the references to the sinners being judged are generic or indefinite.

5. It is theoretically possible that the information about Minos is being given us directly by Dante the Poet speaking to us, as it were, over the head of the Pilgrim; this, however, would run counter to the patterns employed by the poet in his "addresses to the reader." For these patterns, see my article "There is a Place Down There" in *A Dante Symposium,* edited by William de Sua and Gino Rizzo, Chapel Hill, 1965.

6. Note the arresting construction of *stare* with adverb of manner: *Stavvi Minòs orribilmente* . . . "Minos was present there horribly. . . ."

7. No other scholar, to my knowledge, has pointed out the interpolative nature of the two passages in this section (31–36, 40–45) describing the movements (and the screams) of the buffeted souls—as no one has pointed out the same characteristic of the passage describing Minos at work.

8. Some scholars have seen that the *Intesi* must be an indirect reference to Virgil as the source of the Pilgrim's information; others believe it refers to a deduction on the part of the Pilgrim (an incredible explanation of the Pilgrim's ability to arrive at this deduction being offered by Renato Poggioli, "Paolo," pp.315–16). Montano in a note to line 37 leaves the question open: *"Intesi,* non è detto se è Virgilio che

glielo ha detto o una più intima intuizione." (*Storia,* p.403). But even
if the Pilgrim had seen as well as heard the spirits being buffeted by the
winds, how could the manner of their punishment give him "una intima
intuizione" of the nature of their sin the first time he is in the vicinity of
the damned? He has yet to learn the truths of crime and punishment—
for which purpose he is taking this journey.

9. Caretti, who sees somehow together the movements of Minos and
those of the sinners being sentenced, stresses the ternary distribution of
these movements and their "automatic" nature (*Il Canto V,* p.7):

> Ciò che occorre notare è innanzi tutto il veloce ritmo ternario che
> governa i versi 4–15 (Essamina . . . giudica . . . manda . . . ; si
> confessa . . . vede . . . cignesi . . . ; dicono . . . odono . . . son giù
> volte . . .). Quanto è orribile, infatti, la feroce e animalesca
> apparizione di Minosse (*Stavvi Minòs orribilmente, e ringhia*),
> altrettanto angoscioso è quell' inesorabile meccanismo per cui il
> giudizio infernale si svolse davanti ai nostri occhi attraverso una
> serie di gesti evidentemente prestabiliti, se non addirittura auto-
> matici: l'esame delle colpe, l'emanazione delle sentenze, l'esecu-
> zione, e tutto con rigida e infrangibile regola, senza sosta e senza
> possibilità d'evasione (*Sempre dinanzi a lui ne stanno molte:*
> *vanno a vicenda ciascuna al giudizio*).
> Insisto su questo ritmo ternario perché in esso io scorgo soprat-
> tutto il preannuncio ben dissimulato di una delle note essenziali
> del canto: quella della impotenza dei dannati e quella della
> ineluttabilità del giudizio divino.

Strange that one so sensitive to the mood and rhythm of this passage
could believe that the succession of movements described are taking
place on stage before our eyes ("davanti ai nostri occhi").

10. According to my interpretation, the passage describing the sinners
as a group of cranes (46–49) would differ in two regards from the
earlier one (40–43) in which the image of starlings is used: (a) not
only does the first, as has been said, represent graphically-presented information offered by Virgil, while the second alone refers to a formation
actually seen by the Pilgrim; (b) but, whereas the first describes the
totality of sinners (all of whom have been guilty of subjecting reason to
desire), the second presents us with a particular group of the Lustful
characterized by their royal lineage and by the fatal outcome of their lust.
Of the scholars who compare the two passages none has seen the first

of the two contrasts mentioned; as a result they mainly assume that two different bird-formations appear on stage, each representing a sub-division of the totality of sinners. And they are hard put to it to distinguish the one from the other. Poggioli, however ("Paolo," pp.316–318), who takes for granted that only one group is in question, tries to explain the difference between the two descriptions in terms of the Pilgrim's shifting angle of vision.

11. Dido's name will be reserved to be applied later to the group of spirits as a whole seen by the Pilgrim: ". . . la schiera ov'è Dido" (83).

According to Poggioli ("Paolo," p.320), Virgil in his list of names refrains from mentioning Dido out of a sense of modesty since she was a heroine of one of his poems! Later, says Poggioli, when her name is mentioned by Dante (the Pilgrim?), it will be intended as a compliment to the modest Virgil.

12. Compare the well-known summary of Semiramis' vicious career given by Orosius in *Historiarum adversus paganos libri septem* I, 4 (*PL* 31.663–1174). I shall quote a passage from the English translation of Father Roy J. Deferrari (The Catholic University Press, Washington, 1964, pp.22–23):

> This woman, burning with lust and thirsting for blood, in the midst of unceasing adulteries and homicides, after she had slaughtered all whom, summoned by royal command, she had delighted by holding in her adulterous embrace, finally, after shamelessly conceiving a son and impiously abandoning him, and after later having incestuous relations with him, covered up her private disgrace by a public crime. For she decreed that between parents and children no reverence for nature in the conjugal act was to be observed and that each should be free to do as he pleased.

13. It is interesting to note that Helen, who occupies the midpoint in the list, while belonging with the first three named because of her sex, is stylistically differentiated from them in two ways: the "vidi," used to introduce the names of Achilles, Paris and Tristram, is applied first to her; and, while Semiramis is presented as "la prima" and Dido as "l'altra," and Cleopatra is introduced with "poi" ('next')—to Helen the device of listing is not applied. She is not presented as number four of that nefarious group.

14. Since, of the seven sinners named by Virgil, not all had died for love, a number of scholars have suggested that line 69 "che amor di nostra vita dipartille" must be interpreted symbolically; thus, Professor Brandeis (*A Ladder*, p.27): ". . . we must assume that the poet meant that the life of each was spoiled by love—love always as desire dominant over reason. The implication is that love, pitted against reason, inevitably destroys—Helen, who did not die, as much as Tristram; and Paris as much as Dido."

15. The contrast between the grim, bleak atmosphere of the first part of Canto V and the sweetness and light of the second has not been seen by Professor Brandeis, partly because she feels the second element to be already anticipated in the first half of the canto (*A Ladder*, p.25):

> The poetry of the second Circle of the *Inferno* is from its beginning an interplay of opposite elements, paving the way into the two-faced tragic emotion which its dramatic episode is to arouse. In the opening section the atmosphere is a contrast of warring winds and soft, blown figures, of harsh curses and "doleful notes", which the verse supports with its alternation of rushing, bellowing, lashing sounds (28–36) and its passages of dulcet music (40–41, 46–49). The dramatic scene will carry out these contrasts in its counterpoint of passion and pity, of cherishing weakness and destructive power, both generated by love.

Of the images of the starlings and the cranes she says:

> These two bird images do more than tell us how the figures look: they suggest innocence and lightness; they flood the harsh atmosphere with softness, and lure the reader's memory away from the curse against the divine power uttered by these same powerless shadows. The impression the images create will be reinforced by line 73, the pilgrim's first view of Paolo and Francesca as "those two that go together, and seem so light upon the wind"; and further by the image of line 82:

> Quali colombe dal disio chiamate,
>   con l'ali alzate e ferme al dolce nido
>   vegnon per l'aere dal voler portate;

> and ambiguous lightness and ambiguous gentleness will run through all the crucial scene that is to follow.

And in the last paragraph of her chapter she is able to say: "The whole canto is faint with its goal-less sweetness, couched in mellifluous verse, in melting tenderness, in soft images which silence momentarily even the terrible background of tempestuous winds."

But with the references to Paolo and Francesca in line 73 and line 82 we are already in the second half of the canto; there is surely no lightness or softness in the first two bird images. And if Professor Brandeis finds it there it is because she has allowed the later description of Paolo's and Francesca's gliding flight to influence her interpretation of the image of the cranes and, above all, the image of the starlings, that "pandemonium of wings."

It would seem that Professor Brandeis' desire to see the canto as a clear-cut unit has blinded her to the deliberately intended contrast between the two parts.

16. Virgil's suggestion that the Pilgrim should invite the two lovers to descend in the name of "quello amor che i mena" does not seem to have made an impression: at least, in his address to them, the Pilgrim does not mention their love. Professor Brandeis (*A Ladder*, p.27) would bridge the gap by stressing the Pilgrim's "affettuoso grido" (87). But for the Pilgrim to speak lovingly to Francesca and Paolo is hardly the same as to speak to them in the name of their love.

Caretti's procedure (*Il Canto V*, p.20) is to stress the "o anime *affannate*" of line 80. And he believes that when the Pilgrim addresses the lovers in terms of their suffering, he is doing precisely what Virgil had suggested, for the love mentioned by Virgil ("quello amor *che i mena*") was presented as a punishing force.

17. Of the approach of the two lovers to the Pilgrim and his guide Poggioli has this to say ("Paolo," p.325):

> To suggest the action and movement of Paolo and Francesca, Dante introduces here the third and last bird simile of the canto, and compares them to a pair of doves who suddenly abandon the large flock of their kind [!], to rejoin their little ones [!!], and to return to their nest [exclamation marks mine].

18. Both Montano and Brandeis state that the Pilgrim, in his pity, is committing Francesca's sin. The latter scholar defines this (*A Ladder*, p.30) as "the blinding to a greater value by the charm of a lesser," quoting from *Purgatory* XXXI, 34–35.

19. If, disregarding the transitional tercet, we divide the canto into two exact halves (71 + 71) we will see that the first word of the second half is *pietà:* ". . . nomar le donne antiche e' cavalieri,/*pietà* mi giunse . . ." (71–72)

20. It might be said that the Pilgrim's awestruck reaction to the roster of noble names offered him here in Canto V by Virgil is partly excusable since this "roster" follows so soon after the list in Canto IV of illustrious names in Limbo (and nearly all of the former belong also to Antiquity). But the figure of Minos at the entrance to the Second Circle should have made impossible the association in question.

21. Could this insensitivity to connotations also explain the fact that the language of the Pilgrim's appeal (". . . O anime affannate,/venite a noi parlar . . .") must remind us of the consoling words of Christ (*Matthew* XI, 28) : "Venite ad me omnes, qui laboratis, et onerati estis, et ego reficiam vos" ?

22. My belief that the Pilgrim has failed to learn the lesson intended for him is at the opposite pole from that of Caretti. He too sees in the experienced Pilgrim the protagonist of this canto and is intensely concerned with the problem of his moral development. But he believes (*Il Canto V,* p.30) that the Pilgrim has learned his lesson, that he has taken an enormous step forward and that this effort has so exhausted him that, at the end, he collapses. In the short space of time covered by this canto he has come to see that the sweet stirrings of love he knew so well could lead to lust and, that lust, if unrepented, would be punished— must be punished—horribly in Hell. His feelings have run the gamut from horror and fear at what he has witnessed (at first uncomprehendingly), to that of terrible pity for the lengendary lovers of the past (who can, however, no longer be beautiful to him), to the gentler form of pity for the individual Francesca who reminds him of the poignant illusions he once nourished—but which he sees now to be the illusions that they are. And with this he is purged, the catharsis being so painful that he swoons.

But Caretti's sensitive, moving portrayal of the Pilgrim's intense, inner experience—this elaborate analysis, is based on the scantiest of evidence. Only twice are we told specifically of the Pilgrim's reaction and, both times, the reaction is that of pity: "Pietà mi giunse" (72) and

". . . i tuoi martìri / a lagrimar mi fanno . . ." (116–17). The few hints at his feelings that the second half of the canto contains can be variously interpreted, and in the first half there are no hints. Moreover, it is difficult to believe that at the end of his first experience with the damned (and many, many cantos before he will have learned about love from Virgil in Purgatory), the Pilgrim would have achieved a (relative) triumph over himself—and that this triumph would be exemplified by a swoon, by falling upon the floor of Hell!

23. In comparing the attitude of the Pilgrim in *Inferno* V and that of the protagonist of the *Vita nuova* (revealed throughout the work), am I implying that the protagonist of the *Divine Comedy* continues the identity of the latter? To a certain degree this must be the case, for Beatrice at the top of the Mountain of Purgatory addresses the Pilgrim as "Dante" and refers to certain events recorded in the *Vita nuova*. On the other hand one must also, and mainly, think in general of the Pilgrim as Everyman, and one must surely see him as such in the opening line of the *Divine Comedy* ("Nel mezzo del cammin di *nostra* vita").

II: Behold Francesca Who Speaks So Well

1. Two striking exceptions to the tendency to glorify Francesca are represented by the studies of Busnelli ("La ruina del secondo cerchio e Francesca da Rimini," in *Miscellanea dantesca,* Padova, 1922, pp.51–60) and Trombadori ("Saggio critico sull'episodio di Francesca da Rimini" in *Annuario . . . 1927–28 del R. Liceo-Ginnasio M. Foscarini, Venezia*). Trombadori sees Francesca as ". . . la donna demoniaca che la bella persona, gli allettamenti sensuali, adopera ad assopire la virtù del cor gentile e transcinarlo alla perdizione." Busnelli finds in her words ". . . note dolenti, nelle quali fremeranno gli impeti della colpa e della disperazione, l'ostinazione nel pervertimento sensuale, e lo scianto dell'immenso rancore" (p.54). But the two treatments are determined by quite disparate points of view: Busnelli makes no attempt to analyze Francesca's words in any detail nor does he treat her as an individual; she is a paradigmatic figure, representing the unrepentant sinner condemned to Hell. And if her words reveal desperation and perseverance in evil it is because, according to Catholic dogma (Busnelli quotes Thomas Aquinas at greater length than he does Francesca) such are the

characteristics of the state of mind of the damned. To Trombadori, however, she is a figure in her own right and should be seen as the guilty one of the pair of lovers, having seduced the more spiritual Paolo into sin. But the evidence that he offers for his interpretation (an interpretation which Barbi rightly rejects) is highly questionable: for the greater purity of Paolo he can appeal only to the line "Amor, che *al cor gentil* ratto s'apprende" (100) which attributes to Paolo a "cor gentil." And in order to justify his interpretation of the dominant role played by Francesca he was forced to interpret line 103, "Amor, che a *nullo amato amar perdona*" as referring not to herself, as all other critics have assumed, but to Paolo; in other words, she would be saying that the kind of love that seized her demanded that she be loved in turn. But such an interpretation of line 103 would completely destroy the logical consistency of the two tercets (100–105) in which it is embedded.

Between the two extreme interpretations of Francesca there can, of course, be found, especially in recent years, judgments of a more sober, unbiased nature.

2. I believe that Francesca's words "il tuo dottore" refer to Virgil: not to the historical Virgil (whose epic poem she may or may not have read) but simply to the figure she sees accompanying the Pilgrim; Francesca easily could have sensed the monitory role of the Pilgrim's companion ("il tuo dottore") and, knowing that he is a spirit condemned to Hell, who must regret his happier days on earth, she could attribute to him the sad knowledge he must share with her.

3. Once in the *Purgatorio* and again in the *Paradiso* God is called a King: "rege eterno," but in both cases his majesty is indicated within the vast framework of celestial mechanics; he is a Being unapproachable, from whom no individual would solicit a favor for another individual— as Francesca, to judge by her words, would seem to think possible:

> se fosse amico il re de l'universo,
> noi pregheremmo lui de la tua pace. . . .

4. According to Barbi (*Dante,* Firenze, 1952, p.197) the tercet 94–96, containing the words *parlare* and *udire* twice expressed, has been described by G. Vitali as "lungo e inutile preambulo a un discorso che sarà così breve." And the terzina describing Francesca's birthplace as well as the three preceding tercets he considers pleonastic. He, however,

is evidently here voicing criticism of Dante's style, not of Francesca's tendency to loquacity.

5. Poggioli ("Paolo and Francesca: Tragedy or Romance?" *PMLA*, LXXII, pp.328–29), however, suggests that Francesca's *noi* in line 95: "Noi udiremo e parleremo a voi" does not include a reference to Paolo, but is a *pluralis majestatis* (he also interprets the *voi* of the same line as an honorific).

6. It is true that in the last half of the scene with Francesca the Pilgrim himself excludes Paolo from the conversation by addressing himself to Francesca alone.

Incidentally, according to Poggioli "many scholars" have argued that Paolo is indeed given the chance to speak—if only one line: from Francesca's first confession of twenty lines (88–107) they would remove the last one ("Caina attende chi a vita ci spense"), referring to the punishment awaiting the lovers' murderer, to put it into the mouth of the murdered brother. In this way the following line ("Queste parole *da lor* ci fur porte") can be interpreted literally as referring to two speakers and not, as most critics assume, to Francesca who has been speaking for the two of them.

But even though the use of the plural pronoun must be "explained away" if Francesca has been the only speaker (compare also line 109: "Quand'io intesi *quell'anime offense* . . ."), still, what has been proposed to justify the literal interpretation of *da lor* is surely unacceptable: it would imply incredible carelessness on the part of the narrator (who would have failed to announce the change from one speaker to another) ; moreover, if the hitherto mute Paolo would suddenly chime in, this would offer a comically melodramatic conclusion to the deeply moving words of Francesca.

7. The possibility that Francesca might be willing to exploit her own scandal in order to let the Pilgrim realize that he is talking to a well-known person—this apparently does not shock Barbi, who has this to say of the Pilgrim's recognition of Francesca and of his calling her by name (*Dante*, p.196) :

> Quanta tenerezza in quel semplice vocativo premesso ad ogni altra parola! Giunge come il conforto di persona familiare. Il poeta mostra d'essere già stato toccato nel mondo dal caso pietoso di

quella gentile, e riesce a farle subito intendere che partecipa al suo dolore *con l'interesse che si ha per persona ben nota.*

Ercole Di Marco (*Letture dell'Inferno,* ed. V. Vettori, Milano, 1963, pp. 70–71) believes that the *noi* of line 90 (". . . noi che tignemmo il mondo di sanguigno . . .") refers not to all those of "Dido's flock" but only to Francesca and her lover. But not only would this reveal a degree of self-infatuation (of which Di Marco does not seem to be aware) hardly conceivable even in the self-infatuated Francesca: it would imply her belief that the Pilgrim was able to recognize her, which, in turn, would make unnecessary her self-identification by reference to her birthplace.

8. It is not possible that Francesca's latinate construction (". . . il disiato riso / esser baciato . . .") would have been ridiculous even in Latin? Was *legere* one of the verbs that took the *accusativus cum infinitivo?*

9. Barbi (*Dante,* p.202), contesting such critics as Romani and Parodi, believes that Francesca's pronouncements about love are "pur dottrina di Dante"—instead of representing her own transformation of a personal experience into a universal law for the purpose of self-justification.

10. Could the same failure to recognize the extent of her sinfulness also be reflected in Francesca's words: ". . . noi che tignemmo il mondo di sanguigno"? (This line has already been discussed from a stylistic point of view: the "delicacy" of her choice of words.) Perhaps this self-characterization is meant to imply that the only sin committed by those in "Dido's flock" was that of staining the earth with blood.

11. It was said in the previous chapter that Dido's name, not given in Virgil's list of lustful women, was reserved to be applied to the whole group of lustful spirits seen by the Pilgrim (". . . la schiera ov'è Dido"). Actually, it would be more accurate to say that Dido's name is reserved to be applied to Francesca and Paolo: it is only after the Pilgrim's attention has been called to the figures of the two lovers and he has invited them to stop and speak with him, that the phrase in question appears:

Quali colombe dal disio chiamate . . .
vegnon per l'aere dal voler portate

cotali uscir *de la schiere ov'è Dido,*
a noi venendo . . . (82–86)

Why should Dante the Poet wish to remind his reader of Dido just
when Francesca makes her appearance? If we turn to the scene in Book
IV of the *Aeneid* describing the first intimacy of Dido and Aeneas, we
learn that it was Dido who took the initiative in the lovemaking.

12. Caretti (*Il Canto V dell' "Inferno,"* Firenze, 1967, p.35), though
he admits that in her first confession Francesca is confused and seeks
only to justify herself, believes that in the second one she abandons herself to true confession with absolute frankness.

13. Plinio Carli (*Saggi danteschi ricordi e scritti vari*, Firenze, 1954,
pp.3–17), who believes that the love of Paolo and Francesca was pure
at the beginning and would have remained so if they had not revealed
their feelings to each other, is able to see in the reading of the *Lancelot
del lac* "la prima radice del nostro amor" since it marked the beginning
of their love as a shared feeling, and he distinguishes the "nostro amor"
of this line describing their passion from the "amor" mentioned three
times at the beginning of Francesca's confession. The possibility of the
innocent beginnings of the adulterous love of Paolo and Francesca has
also been suggested by Professor Simonelli in Volume 30 of *Studi
danteschi,* Florence (1951), p.235.

14. Certain scholars (Brandeis and Montano) have seen that Francesca was confused as to the relationship between her sin and her punishment, and this is necessarily true of all of those condemned to hell; since
they have not repented, they cannot see their sin for what it truly is. But
the "total confusion" to which I refer involves a network of incon-
sistencies that runs through her confessions from beginning to end.

15. Compare with Grandgent's picture of sin triumphant, as exemplified in Francesca, that of Torraca (*Studi danteschi,* Naples, 1912,
p.427):

> Ah sì, lealmente le ha tenuto fede [Paolo a Francesca]; con lei, tra
> le braccia di lei, morì; fu e sarà con lei, come aveva promesso; onde
> il grido trionfale, che sfida la bufera e l'eternità della pena, e sem-
> brerebbe sfidar il cielo stesso, se non vi si potesse distinguere una
> nota di profonda gratitudine: *Mai da me non fia diviso!*

According to Barbi (*Dante*, pp.180–181) certain scholars (Fedeli Romani and Enrico Corradini) have seen in the treatment of Francesca ". . . persino la glorificazione del talento sulla ragione e la rivendicazione dei diritti dell'umanità contro i divieti della religione."

16. Barbi, for one, in his polemic with Foscolo, ventures the same pessimistic interpretation of the inseparability of the lovers, and mentions the detail of Paolo's tears (*Dante*, p.172).

17. Some scholars, Pagliaro for one (*Saggi di critica semantica*, Messina, 1953, pp.335–55), believe that the *modo* of line 102 (". . . e 'l modo ancor m'offende") refers to the "manner" of Paolo's love for Francesca: she is still "offended" at the thought of his violent passion. The favorite interpretation of those who see Francesca as complaining about the manner of her death is that she regrets having been prevented thereby from repentance. (Cf. Pagliaro for his summary of the different interpretations of this line.)

III: From Measurement to Meaning: Simony

1. De Sanctis (*Lezioni inedite sulla "Divina Commedia,"* ed. M. Manfredi, Naples, 1938, pp.208–9) writes eloquently of the blend of personal passion and objectivity in the tone of this canto. Dante the Poet has allowed his passions to stimulate his genius without betraying any trace of the personal resentment which Dante the man may have felt against his enemy Boniface: "Quanto vi è di personale il genio lo ha consumato, e la passione non serve che ad aguzzare, a rendere sensibilmente ingegnosa la sua fantasia. . . . L'individuo sparisce, l'orizzonte si allarga; e di sotto a Bonifazio esce il papato adultero delle cose sacre."

2. While it is true that any great work of literature reveals more to us each time we read it, so that our comprehension surpasses more and more that of the first reading, still the effect produced on us by the first reading should not be obliterated by the increased understanding: the first impression is also the concern of the poet.

3. Thus the invective against Simon Magus which opens Canto XIX has a far more startling effect than the invective against the Florentines with which Canto XXVI begins: the outburst "Godi Fiorenza" follows directly from the conclusion of the preceding canto.

4. In fact, line 5 ("or convien che per voi suoni la tromba") anticipates the climactic eloquence of Dante the Pilgrim in lines 90–117.

5. Whether it was a baptismal font that Dante broke in his Good Samaritan act, or rather a kind of circular stall within which the priest stood while administering the sacrament of Baptism (thereby protecting himself from the throngs that gathered on Holy Saturday and on Pentecost, the two days of the year set aside for baptism by immersion) has been a matter of great debate, depending to some extent on the interpretation of the word "battezzatori." Since the original baptistry of San Giovanni underwent many changes between the year the church was built and the year of its destruction (1576), and since we have no definite knowledge of the way it looked in Dante's time, all the discussion has been a matter of speculation. For a summary of the opinions expressed, see Luigi Rocca, "Dei quattro pozzetti dell' antico battistero di S. Giovanni in Firenze . . .," *Rendiconte del R. Istituto lombardo di scienza e lettere,* LII, fasc. 13–15, pp.454–469.

6. Cf. Spitzer's article, "An Autobiographical Incident in Inferno XIX," *Romanic Review,* October 1943, pp.248–56. To the problem that most concerns the other commentators—was it a font or a stall that Dante broke?—Spitzer shows a supreme indifference, referring to it in the text of his article as a font and in a footnote as a stall. I should say that it is regrettable that we cannot know the precise image in Dante's mind which he wished to evoke in us by his comparison. But at least we can be sure that Dante must have visualized rising from the wells in the baptistry the figure of a priest erect, using his arms freely as he administers the Holy Sacrament of Baptism; that is, we must see in the protruding, waving legs of the simonists the reversal of the image Dante had in his mind as he recalled the baptistry of his "bel San Giovanni" in Florence. Moreover, Dante surely wished us to think somehow in terms of Baptism (of its implications both for the one administering and the one receiving the sacrament) as we meditate upon the punishment of the simonists: those priests with the greedy hands which once were consecrated to administer that holiest of sacraments, Baptism, the prime example of God's love for his creatures, without which salvation is impossible.

7. The oily surface may remind us of the holy oil placed on the head of the person baptized during the administering of the sacrament of Baptism. Here it would be the feet of those who once administered the holy rite that are, as it were, anointed as a sign of wrath of an all-just "somma Sapienza."

8. The moving flame on the soles of the feet of the sinners should recall to the reader the fulfillment of the promise of baptism "with the Holy Spirit and with fire" (Luke 3:16). On Pentecost the Holy Spirit descended in the form of tongues of fire and rested on the heads of the apostles (Acts 2). According to Tommaseo and also to Sannia (*Il comico . . . nella "Divina Commedia,"* Milan, 1909), the flames licking the feet should recall the red color of the pontifical slippers that the faithful would kiss (p.165). But the flames appear on the feet of all the simonists regardless of their ecclesiastical rank. Sannia may be right, however, in suggesting that the light of the flames recalls the halo of sanctity that the priest might have acquired. And D'Ovidio suggests, in regard to the ensemble of blazing torches represented by the flaming feet: "V'e forse qualcosa di chiesastico in una simile illuminazione, e forse una punta di sarcasmo anche in ciò" (*Nuovi studii danteschi,* Hoepli, Milano, 1907, p.358).

9. One must of course distinguish between the simple "fare motto" and the construction with indirect object "fare motto ad alcuno" ("to salute, greet"). This expression, which does not necessarily refer to the utterance of words, may be used affirmatively (as well as negatively): "Ora avenne un dì che . . . andando il prete . . . per la contrada . . ., cose innanzi, e *fattogli motto,* il domandò dove egli andava." (*Decamerone* VIII, 2)

10. Though amazed, Nicolas does immediately jump to the conclusion that it is Boniface who has addressed him. Sannia (who minimizes the bewilderment of Nicolas) points out (*Il Comico,* p.168) that the words of the Pilgrim, which could be only those of a simple spectator, would not have misled Nicolas if the latter had been able to listen to them calmly and objectively: it was his impatience and eagerness to share his torment with Boniface that led to his false inference. But how could Nicolas, even if he were uninterested in the fate of Boniface,

have thought in terms of "un semplice spettatore curioso"? The inhabitants of Hell were not accustomed to being visited by curious tourists.

11. Against those scholars who assume that the Pilgrim must have guessed immediately that the "Boniface" for whom Nicolas mistook him ("Se' tu già costì ritto, Bonifazio?") was the Pope, Dante's bitterest enemy in this life, D'Ovidio (*Nuovi studii,* p.379) insists that this was impossible. Not only was Bonifazio a common name, but Dante the Pilgrim was, at the moment in question, still ignorant of the identity and the sin of Nicolas. And D'Ovidio adds: "Nè il capovolto aveva detto parola che scopertamente accennasse a un prete, non che a un papa."

12. Of the commentators I have read, Sannia shows the greatest sensitivity to the humor that informs this passage (even if he is a little heavy-handed in expressing his appreciation); unfortunately he is insensitive to the change of tone that marks the beginning of the second half of the canto.

13. Curious indeed is Sannia's reaction to Dante's invective; in his opinion Nicolas was both too vulgar and too wretched to deserve such an elegant attack: he should have provoked in the Pilgrim merely disgust, a silent disdain. Only someone with the stature and the power of Boniface might have inspired such an invective: "Un Bonifazio VIII sicuro e trionfo ci fa scattare nell' invettiva, ma non un Nicolo." (*Il comico,* p.167). At the same time he professes admiration for the Pilgrim's proud refusal to attack Boniface in his own name! Sannia has failed to see the generic implications of this invective, a failure which also prevents him from grasping fully the reason for the Pilgrim's shift from *tu* to *voi* (p.172).

14. It is as though Dante the Pilgrim (who in line 49 "stava come 'l frate che confessa"), after hearing Boniface's confession, now refuses absolution to the Pope!

15. Whereas in *Inferno* V the Pilgrim had failed completely to learn the lesson about Lust that Virgil sought to teach him, here in Canto XIX, with no instruction from Virgil, he has succeeded perfectly in learning the true nature of Simony—from one who had not intended to be his teacher. What a contrast is offered between the figure of the Pilgrim at the end of *Inferno* V, whose torn emotions have brought him to a

complete collapse, and the triumphant figure in Canto XIX, whose poise, whose mastery of the situation, whose righteous anger and cutting eloquence will win for him the accolade of an embrace from Virgil.

16. The biblical reference of Nicolas, capped by the biblical reference of the Pilgrim, is apparently the only one of the rhetorical parallels noted by the commentators.

17. For an interpretation of Canto XXXIV, 79, according to which the antecedent of *elli* would be Lucifer, not Virgil, see the article "Lucifer's Legs" in *PMLA*, June, 1964, by Anna Granville Hatcher and Mark Musa.

IV: At the Gates of Dis

1. See: "Advent at the Gates," *MMLA* I, 1969, 85–93.

By the Second Advent I mean the intermediary coming of Christ according to the medieval conception of the Threefold Coming, the *triplex adventus* of Christ. It is St. Bernard particularly who has elaborated this conception: he tells us that, in addition to the First Coming for the salvation of mankind, and the Final Coming for the judgment of mankind, there is the intermediary advent when Christ comes into the hearts of individuals, of the elect, in order to protect them from temptation and to insure their salvation. By His presence, He enables us to tread Satan under our feet. And whereas in the First Advent He came once and in the Third He will come once, the intermediary advent takes place habitually, daily: ". . . quotidie ad salvandas animas singulorm in spiritu venit" (*PL* CLXXXIII, 40).

2. Chimenz, in his edition of the *Comedy* (Torino, 1962), interprets differently the tercet 19–21 of *Purgatory* VIII:

> Aguzza qui, lettor, ben li occhi al vero,
> ché 'l velo è ora ben tanto sottile,
> certo che 'l trapassar dentro è leggero.

To him *sottile* means 'difficile a interpretarlo allegoricamente' and *trapassar* 'attraversarlo, senza accorgersi del vero ch'esso ricopre.' He objects, that is, to the assumption that Dante is here minimizing the difficulty of the correct allegorical interpretation; he states that if this were true the poet would not have asked us to "agguzzare ben li occhi." But Chimenz, though he refers us to the parallel tercet of *Inferno* IX, has failed to see how the address to the reader in *Purgatory* VIII follows from that of *Inferno* IX. He has overlooked the *ora* which is a reminder of it, and should also be a hint to the reader of what to expect: that is, another angelic advent.

3. If not only Chimenz (see note 2) but the commentators in general have failed to see the intimacy of the relationship between the two addresses to the reader calling upon him for a figurative interpretation, it must be because of the absence of any parallel between the two events that they believe to be offered for this kind of interpretation: the appearance of the Furies in *Inferno* IX, and the appearance of the angels in *Purgatory* VIII.

4. To say that the address to the reader in *Inferno* IX is an admonition to him to find the allegorical meaning of the event that is to follow does not mean that the events that preceded are to be ignored. It is surely significant that the angel representing the First Advent, who comes to save the two travellers, should arrive immediately after the appearance of the Furies and Medusa, representatives of Paganism.

On the plane of the narrative which involves the psychology of the two main actors, the Furies and Medusa represent the Paganism of antiquity, and not in a static way: the Pagan world comes to life not only in the sense that these Pagan creatures play a role in the story but also because what they represent suddenly exerts great influence over Virgil's mind. On the allegorical level it is impossible to prove just exactly what force they symbolize. Among the many suggestions that have been offered we find: evil in general, the hardening of conscience, spiritual blindness and bestiality, malice, fraud, treason, desperation, the sufferings of remorse or the pleasures of the senses.

In trying to determine the allegorical significance for our text of creatures known to mythology one should be able to answer affirmatively two types of questions: 1.) Does the quality attributed them fit into the context of that stage in the story where they appear? 2.) Does such a quality accord with their figures in mythology? Occasionally the answer to both questions is obvious: the savage Minotaur in Canto XII, who guards the Circle of the Violent. In the case of Medusa and the Furies, it is clear, given the multiplicity of suggestions, that the answer to the first question is not obvious; and many of the critics make no attempt to answer the second.

I suggest that they represent Pride and Envy. And if we ask whether Pride and Envy have any connection with Lower Hell, we have only to remember that five of the Seven Deadly Sins (Lust, Gluttony, Avarice, Wrath and Sloth) have already been represented outside of the gates of Dis as so many forms of Incontinence. This leaves only Envy and Pride, which may very well represent the roots of the sins being punished in the abyss of Lower Hell. As for the appropriateness of these qualities for the mythological creatures in question, Medusa's ability to petrify may be compared to the effect of Pride, which according to St. Thomas and others, turns a man's heart to stone. From quite a different point of view the Furies could represent Envy since they themselves were inspired by envy (or served the envious desires of others), if this vice is taken in the sense of Virgil's definition of it in Purgatory: the desire to see the fortunate man brought low. And that the Furies should be here associated with Medusa, the former seeking the latter as their ally, is also compatible with Virgil's description of the two vices as two aspects of the same sin.

5. St. Bernard's definition of the First Coming in terms of the descent into Hell is found in his *First Sermon on the Advents* (*PL, CLXXXIII, 38*):

> Venit utique de corde Dei Patris in uterum Virginis Matris; venit a summo coelo *in inferiores partes terrae* . . . Nunc autem, ut video, et ad terras, et *ad ipsum quoque descendit infernum:* non tanquam vinctus, sed tanquam inter mortuos liber.

I shall discuss the reenactment of the First Advent solely in these terms, since the parallel with our text seems most conspicuous and convincing. My student, however, Professor Denise Heilbronn, has seen also veiled allusions to the Incarnation of Christ; in her unpublished dissertation she points out a number of Marian images suggested by the scene before the gates of Dis, and by the events leading up to it.

6. I cannot agree with those commentators who believe that the function of Phlegyas was to take sinners into his boat, either to transport the Violent and Fraudulent across the Styx to the city of Dis, or to transport the Wrathful to their appointed place of punishment in the Styx itself (and, according to some, to serve as their guardian).

For one thing, if this boat had been used for the transportation of the damned, neither the Pilgrim nor his guide would have been allowed to get in, just as they were not able to enter Charon's boat to cross the Acheron. Secondly, the boat is described as "very small" (*nave piccioletta*) ; thirdly, those who would compare the role of Phlegyas to that of Charon seem to have overlooked the fact that on the shores of the Acheron there was always gathered a huge crowd of the damned, waiting for the boatman, whereas on the shores of the Styx the Pilgrim and his guide meet absolutely no one. Fourthly, since all the sinners in Hell proper are judged by Minos, then hurled below, this would mean that either the Wrathful alone, or the Violent and the Fraudulent along with them, must break their fall on the shores of the Styx, the first to be dropped somewhere within the marsh (at a spot determined by Phlegyas?), the second to be transported to the City of Dis where they start falling once more! Fifthly, Virgil's statement to Phlegyas that they will be with him only long enough to cross the Styx ("più non ci avrai che sol passando il loto" [30]) would make no sense if Phlegyas' sole function were that of regularly transporting souls across (or along) the Styx.

The main argument used in corroboration of the idea that the boat is intended for the damned is the use of *altrui* in describing the travellers' entrance into the boat (VIII, 28–30) :

> Tosto che 'l duca e io nel legno fui,
>   segando se ne va l'antica prora
>   de l'acqua più che non suol con altrui.

The pronoun in line 30 refers, supposedly, to the "others" that Phlegyas is in the habit of transporting, that is, to the damned. But it may very well refer to Phlegyas: the indefinite pronoun is not infrequently found in our poem in reference to a specific individual (or example, the Pilgrim in Canto XXVII asks Guido not to be more stubborn toward him than he had been toward Guido, saying, "Non esser duro più ch'*altri* sia stato").

That Phlegyas has some function is clear from Virgil's indirect indication of the habitual nature of the boatman's activity:

> "Flegïàs, Flegïàs, tu gridi a vòto,"
>   disse lo mio signore, "*a questa volta:*
>   più non ci avrai che sol passando il loto." (VIII, 19–21)

I believe that his function is simply that of guardian: he is in charge of the Wrathful who are punished in the muddy waters of the Styx, and is responsible for seeing that they stay there—much as the devils were the guardians of the Barrators, seeing to it that they stayed in the boiling pitch. Thus Phlegyas would patrol the Styx in his tiny craft to keep the sinners in order. When he sees the two figures standing on the shore he thinks he must restore order by pushing them into the marsh; hence, his threatening words in line 17: "Or se' giunta, anima fella!"—just as one of the devils screamed at the Navarese barrator in Canto XXII (126): "tu se' giunto!" This parallel itself is proof that the formula used in Canto VIII also means "Now I've got you!" and not "at last you have arrived!"—which would be, according to some commentators, a formula of malevolent welcome to the sinners newly arrived on the shore waiting to be transported.

7. The curious scene of the Pilgrim's encounter with Filippo Argenti in which the former expresses such extreme and unmotivated anger, to receive from Virgil the highest tribute of praise recorded in the *Inferno* has baffled many scholars. A most original interpretation has been offered by Heilbronn, who explains in figural terms Virgil's tribute to his ward: she sees in lines 43–45—

> Lo collo poi con le braccia mi cinse;
>   basciommi 'l volto, e disse: "Alma sdegnosa,
>   benedetta colei che 'n te s'incise! . ."—

a combination of two biblical scenes. The gesture is that of Elizabeth embracing Mary; the words are those of the woman in the crowd who was watching Christ cast out devils. For one moment the Pilgrim becomes the vehicle for an allusion to Christ, in order that Virgil may speak the words and carry out the embrace that must remind any reader of the Nativity.

8. Virgil's inability to find the words with which to quell the devils' insolence is all the more ironic because of the fact that he, the eloquent poet of history, had been chosen by Beatrice as her lover's guide precisely because of his eloquence. At the beginning of her plea to Virgil (II, 58–114) Beatrice shows her confidence in his gift of speech:

> Or movi, *e con la tua parola ornata*
>   e con ciò c'ha mestieri al suo campare,
>   l'aiuta, sì ch'io ne sia consolata. (67–69)

She ends with a similar allusion:

> Venni qua giù del mio beato scanno,
> fidandomi *del tuo parlare onesto,*
> ch'onora te e quei ch'udito l'hanno. (112–14)

9. The commentators are divided as to the proper interpretation of the Furies' reference to Theseus: "Mal non vengiammo in Teseo l'assalto!" To some, these words reveal the Furies' regret over their failure to avenge themselves effectively on Theseus ("It is unfortunate that we did not take proper revenge on Theseus for his assault!"). To others the Furies are gloating over their revenge ("We did not revenge badly the assault of Theseus!") That such contradictory interpretations have been offered is perhaps to be explained by the fact that, though Theseus was punished for his assault on Hell by being fastened to a rock in the Lower World—still, according to some traditions, he was later rescued by Hercules. But even though one thinks in terms of a successful vengence wrought by the Furies, the second interpretation is excluded for syntactical reasons: "We did not avenge badly . . ." could have been expressed in Italian only as *non vengiammo mal,* not as *mal non vengiammo. . . .* The use of *mal* "It is unfortunate that . . ." is the same as that in Canto XII, 66: ". . . Mal fu la voglia tua sempre sì tosta!"

10. Though Virgil, when writing the *Fourth Eclogue,* did not understand the hidden truth in his prophecy of the coming of a Savior, those who lived after him could understand—as did Statius who, in *Purgatory* XXII, 70–72, will quote Virgil's own words to him:

> . . . "Secol si rinova,
> torna giustizia e primo tempo umano,
> e progenïe scende da ciel nova."

Compare the last line with Virgil's words in Canto VIII of the *Inferno,* announcing to the Pilgrim the advent of the one who will come to save them (128–30):

> E già di qua da lei discende l'erta,
> passando per li cerchi sanza scorta,
> tal che per lui ne fia la terra aperta.

11. The medieval belief that Virgil was unknowingly prophesying the coming of Christ would represent an exploitation of a Pagan agent

to Christian ends; and we have in the *Inferno* a second exploitation of Virgil the Pagan as agent for a Christian purpose: Virgil's earlier trip through Hell to which he refers in Canto IX, 22-30 and which was an incident invented by Dante—

> Ver è ch'altra fiata qua giù fui,
>   congiurato da quella Eritón cruda
>   che richiamava l'ombre a' corpi sui.
> Di poco era di me la carne nuda,
>   ch'ella mi fece intrar dentr'a quel muro,
>   per trarne un spirto del cerchio di Giuda.
> Quell'è 'l più basso loco e 'l più oscuro
>   e 'l più lontan dal ciel che tutto gira:
>   ben so 'l cammin, però ti fa sicuro.

If Virgil were to be a competent guide through the geography of Hell he must already be familiar with it, and so Dante uses the powers of the Pagan goddess, Erichtho, to give him that familiarity. Heilbronn points out another reason for Dante's invention of Virgil's earlier journey through Hell: it serves as an introduction to what was going to happen to Virgil at the infernal gate. During that first journey he was subject to the powers of Erichtho; at the gate he falls again into the power of Pagan spirits.

We must believe that Virgil made this trip very soon after his death (*Di poco era di me la carne nuda*), probably before Christ's birth and surely before His death on the cross to save mankind—thus, at a time when Pagan forces were still operative. It is true that Virgil in Canto IV (52-54) presents the Harrowing of Hell as having taken place while he was still a novice in Limbo:

> ... "Io era nuovo in questo stato,
>   quando ci vidi venire un possente,
>   con segno di vittoria coronato...."

But stylistic considerations should make it clear that the reference to Erichtho's summons in Canto IX, 25 (*Di poco era di me la carne nuda* ...) points to a time earlier than that of Canto IV, 52: here, where Virgil speaks of his "state," he is thinking in terms of eternity, and his first fifty-two years (Virgil dies nineteen years before the birth of Christ and therefore fifty-two years before the Crucifixion) could well belong to the "new" period of his stay in Limbo. In Canto IX, 25, however, he is timing the event of Erichtho's summons by his death, and if this event had occurred a half-century or more after his death he would hardly have said "Di poco era di me la carne nuda."

Finally, the temporal relationship between Virgil's descent into the very pit of Hell and Christ's Harrowing of Hell is clearly indicated in Canto XII, 34–45:

> Or vo' che sappi che l'altra fïata
> ch'i' discesi qua giù nel basso inferno,
> questa roccia non era ancor cascata.
> Ma certo poco pria, se ben discerno,
> che venisse colui che la gran preda
> levò a Dite del cerchio superno,
> da tutte parti l'alta valle feda
> tremò sì, ch'i' pensai che l'universo
> sentisse amor, per lo qual è chi creda
> più volte il mondo in caòsso converso,
> e in quel punto questa vecchia roccia
> qui e altrove, tal fece riverso.

Thus, the rock which had split in the earthquake announcing the descent of Christ into Limbo had still been intact when Virgil saw it on his mission for Erichtho.

12. It is impossible to overstress the importance of Virgil's failure to use his formula ("Vuolsi così colà dove si puote, / ciò che si vuole, e più non dimandare") which had always been successful, and which was particularly appropriate for the moment he stood before the gates of Dis. Granting that Virgil had to fail in order to make possible the arrival of the *messo,* his failure had taken a form that is utterly inexplicable according to normal psychological laws: it is as if the first sight of the gates of Dis produced in him a temporary state of amnesia—against which we shall see him struggling until he collapses on hearing the Furies' summons to Medusa. The power of those forces of which Virgil is a victim rests heavy on these cantos.

13. There are three ways that Dante allows the cantos of the *Inferno* to end. Sometimes the canto closes with conversation, or with the voice of Dante the Poet. When the canto ends with narration, the final line will serve either to round off the episode of the canto, or to point ahead to that of the next canto. The latter technique, which is the more frequent, may consist of a reference to the start or continuation of movement

ahead, or with an announcement of the point reached—and this last is the case in Canto VII.

14. I have said that the reader's first guess as to the events leading up to the arrival at the tower would be to include only the appearance of the signal-lights, and the brief conversation between the Pilgrim and his guide which this occurrence inspired. This was the interpretation which first occurred to me (and which I long believed), and this has always been the interpretation of my students. As for the commentators, not one that I have consulted attempts to explain just how far back in time the poet intends to go in his "prima che noi fossimo al piè de l'alta torre."

15. In addition to identifying—belatedly, it is true—the tower of Dis with that seen across the river Styx in Canto VIII, Dante offers a dramatic parallel between the two. The first glimpse of the tower in Canto VIII, line 3, is described with the words "Li occhi nostri n'andar suso a la cima"; we have the same ocular process in Canto IX, 35–36:

> però che l'occhio m'avea tutto tratto
> ver' l'alta torre a la cima rovente. . . .

16. In the discussion of the effectiveness of the closing line of Canto VII ("Venimmo al piè d'una torre al da sezzo") there were quoted five other examples of cantos whose closing lines announce "the point reached" by the travellers. One of these has something in common with our line that the other four do not share, for the point reached is the entrance to the next Circle: (VI, 114–115)

> Venimmo al punto dove si digrada:
> quivi trovammo Pluto, il gran nemico.

Canto VI, then, which had been devoted to a description of the Third Circle, ends with the travelers already having arrived at the Fourth Circle—thereby establishing a precedent for the arrival at the gates of Dis in the last line of the following canto. Of course, the opening lines of Canto VII are very different from those of Canto VIII: there is no shift to the past, but rather the smoothest of continuity: we hear in the opening line of Canto VII the voice of Pluto who had been introduced in the last line of Canto VI.

17. There are two other cases which reveal, on careful reading, a play with narrative time that has something in common with the presentation of the arrival at the tower: the arrival of the *messo,* and the entrance into the City of Dis. If the arrival at the tower can be said, *cum grano salis,* to have taken place twice in the narrative, the coming of the *messo* is presented in two installments: in the words of Virgil (VIII, 129–130) predicting his arrival and announcing his approach, and in the narrative of Canto IX (80–81). Thus, in both cases the event that takes place before our eyes has been anticipated; moreover, in both cases, the event anticipated takes place 81 lines after the anticipation. And since, in both cases, the anticipatory words serve to conclude the preceding canto, this means that both events take place in line 81 of their respective cantos.

After his reference to the "men secreta porta" which failed to prevent the entrance of Christ into Hell, Virgil begins his prediction of the coming of the *messo* in the following manner (VIII, 128): *e già di qua da lei discende l'erta /* . . . The description of the thunderous noise suddenly heard in Canto IX that sends the damned ducking for cover in the marsh, begins with the words (64–65):

> *E già* venìa su per le torbide onde
> un fracasso d'un suon pien di spavento. . . .

This stylistic parallel is obviously intended to warn the reader to expect immediately the heavenly messenger. It is also true that the repetition of "e già . . ." underscores the two-beat tempo of the coming of the *messo.*

The parallel between the arrival at the tower and the entrance into the City of Dis is of a different order: the first event is predicted in VII, 130, and is one that happened "too soon" according to the normal pace of the narrative; the entrance into the City of Dis predicted in Canto IX, 106, involves an event that occurs later than it should have, according to the normal laws of the narrative that had operated up to the point when Virgil sees the gates of Dis. I have said that if Virgil had then used his formula, he and his ward would have entered the gates in Canto VIII, a few lines after the devils' challenge: "Chi è costui . . .?" (84–85) —perhaps in line 89. But because the poet of the *Divine Comedy* wished to bring on stage the *messo,* Virgil had to fail, and the entrance through the gates was postponed until Canto IX, 106. Curiously enough, it is precisely in line 89 of Canto IX that the *messo* comes to the gates: "Venne a la porta, e con una verghetta / l'aperse. . . ." Thus, the equivalent of a whole canto lies between the travellers' failure to enter through the gates in Canto VIII, 89, and the opening of the gates due to a divine intervention made necessary by Virgil's failure.

18. It has already been stressed in this chapter that Virgil had to fail before the gates of Dis in order that the *messo* could be sent (in order that the First Advent could be represented). Since he failed, the angel had to come for the sake of the Pilgrim, but the reader knows that the success of the Pilgrim's journey was guaranteed from the beginning; nothing actually could have prevented him from reaching his goal. And so, as a faint anticipation of this inevitability Dante would end Canto VII with the lines beginning tranquilly: "Così girammo . . . ," and ending with the announcement of arrival.

Of course, at the end of Canto VII, the Pilgrim has arrived only at the gates. The crucial difficulty (for the hostility of Phlegyas and Filippo Argenti were of minor importance) still awaited him on his arrival. But the Pilgrim has arrived at the gate through which he will pass; Dante the Poet brought him there in one line, knowing the *messo* must come to let him through.

V: In the Valley of the Princes

1. Toward the beginning of Canto IX the Pilgrim, overcome by weariness of the flesh, lies down on the grass to sleep and he is visited by a dream which he himself suggests may be prophetic. He sees an eagle poised in the sky with feathers of gold. As he lies waiting for the bird to swoop down, he thinks that he must be in the same place where Ganymede was when he was taken up to the gods. And he thinks to himself that it must be always at this spot and no other that this eagle is accustomed to strike. After wheeling awhile the eagle descends, terrible as lightning, and catches him up to the region of fire where both burn together. It is true that the dreams from which the second hymn asks for protection are those sent by the devil, whereas the Pilgrim's dream was evidently sent by God, but it can be no coincidence that after listening with rapt attention to a hymn begging protection from "somnia / et noctium fantasmata," the Pilgrim has his phantasmagoric dream.

2. Obviously, all hymns are written for the living, but not all are so limited to daily living as is the *Te lucis ante.* The psalm *De exitu,* sung by

the newly-arrived souls just freed from their earthly exile, could easily remind the reader of their new non-earthly existence; and the *Miserere,* pleading for purification, could well be sung by souls anticipating the purgation of their sins. It is also true that the hymns sung by those in Purgatory proper suggest nothing that jars with the stage they have reached in their journey to God—except for the last part of the *Pater noster* which the Pilgrim, having just entered the gates of Purgatory, hears recited. But he also hears the group (XI, 22–23) remind God of the irrelevancy for them of the last lines: "Quest' ultima preghiera, segnor caro, / già non si fa per noi, ché non bisogna. . . ."

3. There is, however, one thing in common between the condition of the souls in the valley (and, indeed, in the ante-Purgatory as a whole) and that of Christians in this world. Though their exile on earth is ended, they are still exiled from Heaven and even from preparation for Heaven. In a sense the words *exsules, exilium,* apply also to them, and the nostalgic tone of the hymn may well reflect the mood of those who sing it outside the gates of Purgatory.

4. Curtius (*European Literature and the Latin Middle Ages,* New York, 1953) in his treatment of the "Ideal Landscape," Chapter 10, does not mention the Garden in *Purgatory* XXVIII or, in fact, any such description in vernacular writers, but according to the formula which he offers for description of the "Pleasance" (p.195) from the Empire to the sixteenth century, Dante's description fulfills the requirements ideally.

> It is, as we saw, a beautiful, shaded natural site. Its minimum ingredients comprise a tree (or several trees), a meadow and a spring or brook. Birdsong and flowers may be added. The most elaborate examples also add a breeze.

5. The possibility that Sordello, compared to a couchant lion, may represent the Lion of Judah was pointed out by Scartazzini-Vandelli. Since the biblical reference to the tribe of Judah described as a young, couchant lion, has been understood in the Judeo-Christian tradition as Messianic prophecy, Heilbronn, in her dissertation, sees a suggestion of Christ in the figure of Sordello.

6. The passage describing the Princes in the Valley is not the only one in which a group of individuals are presented by name to the

reader: one thinks immediately of the roll-call of the great shades in Limbo. But though these are identified and often commented upon, there is only one whose figure is clearly outlined before us. That is the founder of the Roman Empire: "Cesare armato con li occhi grifani."

7. Sordello's presentation of the Princes gives something of the effect of a double focus, because the individual figures whom he outlines for the reader had already been presented as amorphous elements of an anonymous mass of souls singing hymns, who continue to sing as Sordello speaks. But a third element is added to the picture by Sordello himself: as he points out the Princes in the valley he mentions their successors who are still alive (and who, in general, are far inferior to them). Thus we see Ottocar who seems to be comforting the Emperor Rudolph and we are reminded of Wenceslaus, his son, who battens on wantonness and ease.

8. Conrad, invited enthusiastically by Nino in lines 65–66 to come and meet the living pilgrim, does not address him until line 112 (in the meantime, however, never taking his eyes from him) ; it could be that both his hesitation and his steady gaze were due to his fascination at the miracle of the Pilgrim's presence among the dead.

And his delay is the last in a small series of postponements that have been introduced into the narrative. Twice Sordello is slow in performing an act which had been prepared for by the context: having proposed in lines 46–48 of Canto VII to lead the two travellers to join the souls in the valley, he delays this meeting in order to first present the Princes from a distance; the meeting actually takes place in Canto VIII, 46–48— that is, after an interval of exactly (what might be called) one canto's length. Earlier, Sordello, asked by Virgil in Canto VI, 67–68, for directions to climb the Mountain, ignores the request in his eagerness to learn more about the two strange travellers; it is only when Virgil repeats his request in the next canto (37–39) that Sordello accedes to it by offering himself as guide. There are two other postponements, and on another plane, where it is the author himself who chooses to hold back from us information that might have come much sooner. The less conspicuous involves the slow-motion presentation to view of the souls in the valley singing Salve regina—the effect being prolonged by Sordello's delayed descent into the valley where they are. And of course, there is the dramatic device of "interruption" by which the poet postpones the conclusion of the embrace between Virgil and Sordello. In every case the motivation, psychological or aesthetic, of the postponement is clear.

But, though none of the cases is puzzling in itself, there is a need to explain the frequent recurrence of the same device. I suggest that it is intended as a leit-motif reminder of the reason for the presence of the Princes in the ante-Purgatory—which is, of course, the reason for the presence there of all the rest. Nowhere in the scenes just described is any statement made about the all-important fact that these souls, like the rest, have been excluded from Purgatory proper because of their postponement of repentance (which, in turn entails the postponement of their expiation). And so, Sordello and Conrad are made to "imitate" the action that brought them to the ante-Purgatory. Dante the Poet, too, on another plane, has reflected the same tempo of delay. And as for the fact that for each single case it is possible to find a convincing explanation, this is simply the sign of great artistry.

9. On the two occasions when the Pilgrim stops listening to the words of a speaker (to Virgil's words in the *Inferno*, to Sordello's words in *Purgatory*), we are meant, of course, to assume that the speaker continues: that is, he goes on uttering words that are not reported. This is stated explicitly in the first instance ("E altro disse, ma non l'ho a mente"). As for Sordello's words, the last lines that we have surely suggest nothing of a conclusion; the details offered about Guiglielmo of Monferrato could easily have been followed by the identification of a tenth ruler, or an eleventh (as if one could go on forever talking about the woes of Europe). The fact that Sordello's words, as recorded, bring the canto to an end, produces a special effect lacking in the first case: those words we do not hear must have been spoken in the interval between two cantos.

VI: The "Sweet New Style" That I Hear

1. According to Casella (*Studi danteschi*, XVIII, 1934, p.108) Dante's words: "I' mi son un che . . ." may have been inspired by Richard of St. Victor, a mystic well known to Dante:

> Quomodo enim de amore loquitur homo qui non amat, qui vim non sentit amoris? De aliis nempe copiosa in libris occurrit materia; hujus vero aut tota intus est aut nusquam est, quia non ab ex-

terioribus ad interiora suavitatis suae secreta transponet, sed ab interioribus ad exteriora transmittit. Solus proinde de ea digne loquitur qui secundum quod cor dictat interius exterius verba componit. (Migne, *PL* 196, 1195)

2. Up until the present I have always referred to the protagonist of the *Divine Comedy* as the "Pilgrim" (not as "Dante")—for the obvious reason of avoiding a confusion between this character and his creator. Here, in my statement "[Bonagiunta] applies Dante's description of his method to other poets . . ." this practice has been abandoned—again, for obvious reasons. While Bonagiunta surely sees in our protagonist a pilgrim on his journey toward God (he has recognized the miracle of this presence on his terrace), the remarks that he addresses to him show his deep concern with the historical figure that the Pilgrim represents to him: that political figure who will soon go into exile as well as the poet who wrote "Donne ch'avete . . ." and other love lyrics. Accordingly, in this chapter I shall often call our Pilgrim by his historical name.

Incidentally, "Dante the Poet," who must absolutely be distinguished from the Pilgrim, is not simply the historical Dante who happened to write the *Divine Comedy,* as he also happened to write a number of other works: he is, for the reader of the *Divine Comedy,* a mystic presence, an eternal presence, in the text, whose voice we are allowed to hear from time to time.

3. Compare, in Grabher's edition of the *Divine Comedy* (Milano, 1965), the rather sentimental observation about Nella, Piccarda and Gentucca, the three virtuous ladies:

. . . ma di fronte a malvagi come Corso Donati che fanno maledire la vita (v. 82 sgg.) ecco rievocate in questo stesso cerchio e Nella (*Purg.,* XXIII, 87 sgg.) e Piccarda e questa dolce creatura che, senza esser santa come Piccarda, è pur essa una chiara luce sulla terra, con la sua velata promessa di bontà per l' esule sbattuto dagli uomini e dalla sorte.

There is also a reference in Canto XXIII to ladies lacking in virtue: Forese, reminded of the sweet purity of his Nella points to the contrast offered by the brazen hussies of Florence, delivering a savage indictment against those women who go ". . . mostrando con le poppe il petto." And, thinking now in terms of unchaste women, one cannot fail to be reminded of the Siren who, at the beginning of this the third day (Canto XIX), visits the Pilgrim in a dream, his second dream on the Mountain of Purgatory: the stammering, cross-eyed, club-footed female, first made beautiful by the Pilgrim's imagination, then revealed in her true hideousness when Virgil pulls off her garment and the stench awakens the Pilgrim. This dream is surely occasioned by the disquisition on love that he had heard from the lips of his teacher in the preceding two cantos.

4. Though nothing is explicitly stated about the virtue of Gentucca, we know enough about Dante's opinion of the sinfulness of Lucca to see that if one of its inhabitants were able to so compensate for the sins of the other Lucchesi as to make this city pleasurable for the poet, her virtue, indeed, must be superlative.

The lack of explicit reference to Gentucca's virtue is perhaps the reason why the thematic connection between Bonagiunta's "praise of a virtuous lady" and Dante's *canzone* in praise of Beatrice has been overlooked even by those critics who have seen that the *canzone* in question was quoted precisely because of its theme of unselfish praise. And as for the critics who see in Bonagiunta's prophecy reference to a future love afflair awaiting the author of the *Divine Comedy* (!) what is there to say?

5. J. E. Shaw ("Dante and Bonagiunta," *Annual Report of the Dante Society,* 1936, pp.1–18) is the only scholar to my knowledge who interprets *ch'i' odo* literally: ". . . and there is no doubt that here *ch'i' odo* refers to the words that Dante has just spoken" (p.16). But his following remarks become more and more disconcerting:

> So in our passage, it is not unlikely that Dante's words:
>
> I' mi son un, che quando
> Amor mi spira, noto, e a quel modo
> ch'e' ditta dentro, vo significando.
>
> are to be taken as an example of the new style that Bonagiunta admires. They are worth attention for their beauty as well as their meaning. The sentence is dignified and limpidly clear, the construction, though clear, is not childish like "Petrus amat multum dominam Bertam": It is a "constructio elata", the main sentence including two subordinate adverbial sentences. The words . . . are smooth-sounding: except the double *t* of *ditta,* and the unvoiced *sp* of *spira,* the only combination of consonants are those of which one at least is a sonant . . . I am not sure that Dante would have classed them as belonging to the tragic style . . .

But apart from the rather pedantic analysis of the style of Dante's tercet (and the rather patronizing tone of the praise) Shaw's words suggest that Dante is putting on a performance for Bonagiunta, improvising, on the spot, a sample of the style that Bonagiunta admired. Surely it is the *meaning* of these words to which Bonagiunta responds with such enthusiasm—as we shall have more reason to see later on.

Why have not more commentators seen that the words ". . . dolce stil novo ch'i' odo . . ." could not possibly refer to a corpus of poetic compositions? Because they have believed this corpus to be that of a group of poets, they have sought to find a formula, suggested by Dante's "I' mi son un che . . . ," which could be applied to an ensemble of poems as different from each other as "Questa rose novella . . . ," "Donna mi prega . . ." and "Donne ch'avete . . ." No wonder if the descriptions of the *dolce stil novo* have ranged from (what I have called) a rather silly emphasis on pure, effortless lyricism to a pedantic insistence on scholastic tendencies.

6. We may also note the use of *chi'i odo* in *Purg.* XXVI, 106–108. Guinizzelli, hearing the Pilgrim's words addressed to the group of the Lustful, says to him,

> . . ."Tu lasci tal vestigio
> (per quel ch'i' odo) in me, e tanto chiaro,
> che Letè nol può tòrre né far bigio."

Here "the effect of sublime words on an impressionable listener" is explicitly stated.

7. Bonagiunta's question which seems to inquire into the identity of the Pilgrim (though he must have already recognized him, since he has prophesied about him) has been the subject of much scholarly debate, which is admirably summed up by Shaw ("Dante," pp.3–6).

8. That the idea expressed in the canzone mentioned by Bonagiunta represents a turning point in Dante's love for Beatrice, is taken for granted by all critics of the *Vita nuova*—perhaps too easily. For it is also true that after having taken the new road Dante was capable more than once of wandering away from it before the account of his *New Life* ends. (See the "Essay . . ." in my *Dante's "Vita nuova,"* Indiana University Press, 1973.)

9. That the Pilgrim has thoroughly absorbed Virgil's teachings about the various kinds of love is suggested in a very subtle way by a certain verbal parallel. Virgil in *Purgatory* XVII had described the "altro ben" which does not make men happy:

> Altro ben è che non fa l'uom felice;
> non è felicità, non è la buona
> essenza, d'ogne ben frutto e radice.
> L' amor ch'ad esso troppo s'abbandona
> *di sovr' a noi si piange per tre cerchi;*
> ma come tripartito si ragiona,
> tacciolo, acciò che tu per te ne cerchi. (133–139)

Two cantos later, after the Pilgrim has awakened from his dream about the loathsome Siren and informed Virgil of a "novella vision" that he has had, his teacher, who knows what he must have dreamed, asks:

> "Vedesti," disse, "quell'antica strega
> *che sola sovr' a noi omai si piagne;*
> vedesti come l'uom da lei si slega. . . ." (XIX, 58–60)

Thus, it is clear that the Siren of the Pilgrim's dream is in truth the "altro ben" described by Virgil.

Incidentally, the Siren, the "dolce serena" turned hideous, serves as a connecting link between Virgil's words on love in XVII–XVIII and the chaste and unchaste women of XXIII–XXIV.

10. For a similar idea concerning the larger implications of Dante's poetic *credo* ("I' mi son un che . . .") see Francis Fergusson, *Dante's Drama of the Mind,* Princeton University Press (1953), pp.152–153.

11. Evidently Bonagiunta had spent his time on this terrace in the way recommended to gluttons by Rabanus Maurus in his *Remedia contra morbum gastrimargiae* . . . (PL, CXII, 1370) : ". . . mentemque suam contemplationi divinae defigat amore virtutum potius et pulchritudine caelestium delectetur, et ita velut caduca despiciet universa praesentia." In the last two lines of Bonagiunta's comparison of Dante's poetic procedure with his own and that of da Lentino and Guittone ("E qual più a riguardare oltre si mette / non vede più da l'uno a l'altro stilo") he can hardly be saying that from the point of view of literary style, as this is conventionally conceived, there is no difference between that of Dante and that, for instance, of Guittone d'Arezzo. Probably he meant that the

stylistic differences that did exist were relatively unimportant in comparison with the great gulf that separates a poet who has Dante's conception of Love from one who does not; that is, he has learned the lesson of *I Corinthians* 13, 1:

> Si linguis hominum loquar, et angelorum, caritatem autem non habeam, factus sum velut aes sonans aut cymbalum tinniens.

Similarly, it might be said that Dante, when he was able to write "Donne ch'avete intelletto d' amore," had learned the lesson of verse 11 of the same chapter:

> Cum essem parvulus, loquebar ut parvulus, sapiebam ut parvulus, cogitabam ut parvulus; quando autem factus sum vir evacuavi quae erant parvuli.

Finally, one may note the rather close correspondence between the (negatively described) attributes of *caritas* listed in I *Cor.* 13, verse 4: ". . . caritas non aemulatur, non agit perperam, non inflatur . . ." and the sins discussed by Virgil in *Purgatory* XVII, all of them due to the wrong kind of Love, the lack of *caritas*.

Incidentally, Shaw would paraphrase lines 61–62 ". . . and no one, not even the most penetrating expert, sees a greater difference between the two styles than I" ("Dante," p.18). That is, Bonagiunta would be stressing, not belittling, the stylistic difference.

12. Shaw is the first, apparently, to have seen in Bonagiunta's words (49–51) the sign of the spiritual development he has undergone as a penitent on the terrace of the Gluttons.

13. Nor can one compare Bonagiunta's praise of Gentucca to the more deep-felt and moving words of Forese—who is given two opportunities to develop the theme of praise—for, whereas Bonagiunta's words would reveal a decision to choose the theme in question, those of Forese represent simply an answer to factual questions asked of him by the Pilgrim—concerning the two ladies whom he loved most on earth.

14. Cf., however, the "Dizionario della *Divina Comedia,* a cura di Michele Messina," Florence, 1954, in which our passage is listed under *penne* 'wings' (line 54 being interpreted: "volate a fianco di Amore [che vi detta dentro . . .]"). Singleton, too, in the first edition of *An Essay on the "Vita nuova,"* Cambridge, 1949 (p.93), translates *penne* as

'wings'—only, unfortunately, to revert to the traditional interpretation in his second edition.

15. The strange effect of predicating movement-through-space on the part of the "pens" is usually mitigated by the translators' choice of a verb more abstract in meaning than *andarsene* (e.g. 'follow' which suggests 'compliance').

16. The cautious wording "anatomical reference" (instead of simply "wings") used of the meanings of *penne* in the *Divine Comedy* is due to the special sense of *penne* in *Inferno* XX, 45.

17. Since the Pilgrim's request to Arnaut Daniel appears as indirect discourse in the narrative:

> E dissi ch'al suo nome il mio disire
> Apparecchiava grazïoso loco.

we shall never know whether he actually said ". . . al *tuo* nome" or ". . . al *vostro* nome"!

18. Incidentally, Bonagiunta changes his mode of address to Dante twice: before ending with "voi" he passes (49) from the casual "tu" of the beginning to the impersonal ". . . colui che . . ." (echoed in Dante's response: "I' mi son *un che* . . ." with its suggestion of historical import).

19. Not that there is anything necessarily unpoetic in a metaphoric reference to pens: note the vivid image of the pen in the *Epistola ad Severinum de caritate,* already cited, of Richard of St. Victor:

> Ne mireris igitur si alium audire de hac mallem quam loqui ipse. Illum, inquam, audire vellem qui *calamum lingue tingeret in sanguine cordis,* quia tunc vera et veneranda doctrina est cum quod lingua loquitur conscientia dictat, caritas suggerit, et spiritus ingerit.

It is a curious coincidence that this passage follows immediately after the one quoted in note 1 as a possible source of Dante's words "I' mi son un che. . . ." At first glance this might seem to be evidence in favor of the traditional interpretation of *penne* as 'pens': if, for the Pilgrim's answer to Bonagiunta, Dante borrowed from the *Epistola* the "Solus . . . [de Amore] digne loquitur qui secundum quod cor dictat verba componit," is it not natural to suppose that, for Bonagiunta's (immediately following) reply to Dante, he would also be borrowing the image of the "pen" in the passage that immediately follows in the *Epistola?*

Surely there would have been nothing strange in such a procedure on his part, whether taking over the image intact, or modifying it. We can be sure, however, that in the latter case the modification would not have consisted in replacing the most forceful image in the whole treatise ("to dip the pen of the tongue into the blood of the heart") by the very blurry "image of the pens" that the translators offer.

20. The image of the wingèd soul flying upward to higher stages of virtue and understanding is one, incidentally, that was dear to the heart of Richard of St. Victor. A favorite metaphor of his was that of *penna contemplationis*—which surely in the passages cited below is not to be translated 'the *pen* of contemplation'! We find in *De Trinitate* (*Textes philosophiques du moyen âge,* VI, Paris, 1958):

> Quando ad sublimium et invisibilium investigationem et demonstrationem nitimur, similitudinum scala libenter utimur, et habeant qua ascendere possint qui *contemplationis pennas* nundum acceperunt. In illa itaque natura quam ad divinam imaginem et similitudinem factam agnovimus, divinum simile libenter querimus et elicimus, unde ad divinorum intelligentiam sublevari valeamus. (*Caput* XXVI, p.261)

> Sed singulare donum et pre omnibus praecipuum, usque ad hoc celum *penna contemplationis* volare et intellectuales oculos ejus radiis infigere. (*Prologus,* p.83)

and in *De IV gradibus violentae caritatis* (*Textes philosophiques du moyen âge III,* Paris, 1955):

> Hanc gratiam (i.e. of seeing what the eye has never seen, etc.) acceperant et *penna contemplationis* volabant quos propheta mirando intuebatur et intuendo mirabatur . . . (para. 34, p.161)

Of special interest is the following passage from *De Trinitate* in which the "ascendamus *post* caput nostrum" cannot fail to recall the *"di retro al dittator sen vanno strette"* of Bonagiunta's image:

> Si filii sumus Syon, sublimen illam contemplationis scalam erigamus, assumamus *pennas ut aquile,* in quibus nos possimus a terrenis suspendere et ad celestia levare. Sapiamus que celestia sunt, *non que super terram, ubi Christus est ad dexteram Dei sedens.*

Sequamur quo Paulus precessit, qui usque ad tertii celi secreta
volavit...

Ascendamus post caput nostrum . . . Ascendamus igitur spiri-
tualiter, ascendamus intellectualiter, quo iterim non licet corpo-
raliter. (*Prologus*, p.82)

Boethius in *De consolatione philosophiae*, Liber IV, 1, has Lady Philoso-
phy refer to her guidance in the following terms:

> Et quoniam verae formam beatitudinis me dudum monstrante
> vidisti, quo etiam sita sit, agnovisti, decursis omnibus, quae prae-
> mittere necessarium puto, viam tibi, quae te domum revehat,
> ostendam. Pennas etiam tuae menti, quibus se in altum tollere
> possit, adfigam, ut pertubatione depulsa sospes in patriam meo
> ductu, mea semita, meis etiam vehiculis revertaris.

> Sunt etenim pennae volucres mihi,
> quae celsa conscendant poli;
> quas sibi cum velox mens induit,
> terras perosa despicit,
> aeris immensi superat globum
> nubesque postergum videt.
> quique agili motu calet aetheris,
> trascendit ignis verticem,
> donec in astriferas surgas domos
> Phoeboque coniungat vias
> aut comitetur iter gelidi senis
> miles corusci sideris,
> vel, quocumque micans nox pingitur,
> recurrat astri circulum
> atque, ubi iam exhausti fuerit satis,
> polum relinquat extimum
> dorsaque velocis premat aetheris
> compos verendi luminis...

Augustine speaks several times of the necessity for the winged soul to
have God as his guide.

> Nam et cum pennis meis casura sum, nisi tu deducas. Ergo alas
> habent bonas et liberas, et nullo visco obligatas, animae bene ope-
> rantes praecepta Dei, habentes charitatem de conscientia pura et
> fide non ficta (I *Tim.* 1, 5). Sed quantumvis sint praeditae virtu-
> tibus charitatis, quid ad illam dilectionem Dei, qua sunt dilectae,
> etiam eum visco essent implicatae? Major ergo in nos dilectio Dei,
> quam nostra in illum. Nostra dilectio pennae nostrae sunt: sed ille

ambulat et *super pennas ventorum.* —*Psalm* CIII: PL 37, 1347–1548.

. . . Opus ergo est ut habeamus pennas, et opus est ut ipse deducat; adjutor enim noster est . . . —*Psalm* CXXXVIII, 13: PL 37, 1792.

21. That it was the Pilgrim's reference to Beatrice, overheard by Bonagiunta, that made it possible for the Luccan poet to learn Dante's identity is the suggestion of Shaw ("Dante," p.2).

22. Wingèd flight and bringing forth words of praise, are these not seen together by Bonagiunta? Before referring to the wings of Dante flying straight behind Love, the Luccan poet first presents Dante as "bringing forth" words of praise (lines 49–50), and we cannot fail to see the prominent position of the word *fore* in 49 (". . . . Ma dì s'i' veggio qui colui che fore / trasse le nove rime . . ."), put into relief not only by its end position in the line but also by the reversal of normal word order *fore / trasse* (emphasized by the enjambment). And perhaps the two ideas are condensed in Dante's phrase of self-description, ". . . *vo significando.*"

Close readings of five cantos in the *Divine Comedy* have yielded brilliant and imaginative new interpretations of Dante's great work by a critic who draws upon his experience as teacher and translator of Dante. Each of the book's six chapters shows the continuity of Dante's basic theme from the early to the later work: the process of education of the human soul as it learns to transcend selfhood and proceed toward an understanding of God. The cantos chosen for analysis offer excellent examples of Dante's narrative skill and his art of characterization, aspects of Dante's genius which Musa treats with particular sensitivity.

The first and second chapters are devoted to three neglected aspects of Canto V: the canto's structure, the significant role played by the Pilgrim, and Dante's intention with respect to Francesca da Rimini. For centuries readers have been spellbound by the charming figure of Francesca, but Musa shows that Dante's intention was to present her as guilty and self-deluding, to be seen in the light of the Hell described in the first half of the canto. His interpretation restores the balance of Canto V by placing greater emphasis on the Pilgrim's reaction to the Second Circle of Hell. In his third essay Musa shows that Canto XIX of the *Inferno* is distinguished by the intensity of moral anger it reveals and the artistry by which the canto's structure sets in relief the Pilgrim's moral lesson.